Special Issues from the *Teachers College Record*

JONAS F. SOLTIS, Series Editor

THE CARE AND EDUCATION OF YOUNG CHILDREN

Expanding Contexts, Sharpening Focus

Frances O'Connell Rust
Leslie R. Williams

Editors

Teachers College, Columbia University
New York and London

Published by Teachers College Press, 1234 Amsterdam Avenue
New York, NY 10027

Originally published in *Teachers College Record*, v. 90, no. 3, Spring 1989.

Library of Congress Cataloging-in-Publication Data

The Care and education of young children.

  (Special issues from the Teachers College record)
  "Originally published in Teachers College record, v. 90, no. 3, Spring 1989"—CIP t.p. verso.
  Includes index.
  1. Child care services—United States. 2. Child welfare—United States. 3. Early childhood education—United States. I. Rust, Frances O'Connell. II. Williams, Leslie R., 1944- . III. Series.
HQ778.7.U6C36 1989   362.7   89-4548

ISBN 0-8077-2984-1 (pbk. : alk. paper)

Printed on acid-free paper.

Manufactured in the United States of America

96 95 94 93 92 91 90 89   8 7 6 5 4 3 2 1

Contents

Introduction

FRANCES O'CONNELL RUST
Manhattanville College
LESLIE R. WILLIAMS
Teachers College, Columbia University

Early childhood education and child care are two now highly visible aspects of a field of study, research, and practice focusing on the young child. That field, commonly referred to in a growing body of literature as "early childhood," has in the past encompassed many distinct specializations, including study of the development of young children from birth to age eight, provision of child-care services, nursery school and kindergarten education, after-school programs, study and guidance of parenting, specialized caregiver and teacher preparation, and a variety of advocacy activities.

For nearly two hundred years, the field has grown and changed as young children have become increasingly precious and important to our society. Currently, however, the field is undergoing the most rapid expansion of its concerns and redefinition of its purpose in its long history. While there have been other periods of high activity concerning the well-being of young children in the United States (as in the inception of the Head Start program in the 1960s), the present form of attention given to early childhood is distinguishing itself in two ways. It is becoming more broadly based, with heightened awareness of the powerful intersection of social, economic, and political forces affecting the lives of young children and their families. At the same time, there is a greater focus on the issues cutting across all those spheres that affect the nurturance of our youngest citizens, and across the specializations within the field. What have been considered separate strands of endeavor are now being woven into whole cloth.

The concerns of early childhood are more far ranging than ever before partly because of the age span of the children served by the field. Although three-, four-, and five-year-old children were the subjects of much of the pioneer work in the field, infants and toddlers (neonates to age three) and primary school children (six- to eight-year-olds) have recently represented important extensions of our study, research, and practice. With the acceptance of the total continuum from birth through the third grade as our province has come an equally great expansion of the settings in which the work of early childhood practitioners and researchers is carried out. These settings now range from the infants' own homes or homes of other caregivers to informal and formal public and private school classrooms, as well as a variety of nonschool situations, such as work place or employer-provided facilities, and hospital and hospice programs.

Parents, caregivers, family and social workers, health-care professionals, and teachers have all become key players in the services having an impact on children's lives. Once focusing more singularly on *care* or *education*, these players are now converging in recognition of the commonality of their concerns. Today, high-quality child care assumes the provision of educational opportunities across the age range served. Programs originally designed as educational have been expanded to include important elements of care, that is, provision of nutritional and social services, and extended or full-day options. We are presently faced with an almost exponential increase in demand for services at the same time the knowledge base undergirding our work is being reassessed for its adequacy in addressing such varied expectations.

This new collection of essays represents some of the most recent thinking on the conceptual and practical growth within the field. It examines three interconnected facets of the larger involvement, namely, the broad sociocultural contexts influencing the development of young children and their families, the evolution of specific settings or programs where care and education occur, and the emerging consciousness of early childhood educators and care providers toward their responsibility for refinement of practice. The chapters are grouped and sequenced to reflect these topics.

The first five chapters provide a view of the broad context in which current concerns over early childhood are evidenced in our society. Senator Moynihan begins with a political and social plea to artfully create policies to serve our children. Edelman follows with an equally sensitive concern for the child, the family, and the nation from an economic point of view. Despite our attempts to desegregate and integrate the various racial and ethnic groups comprising our society, black children (and others identified as "minorities") still suffer social and educational inequities. Comer would make the overcoming of racism a special purpose of the early childhood field. Schorr identifies a broad array of factors that put young children at risk and describes programs that have been successful in dealing with them. Lee expands the examination of context further to the theoretical stance we take toward the child's mind. He addresses the question of egocentricity versus sociocentricity in the young child.

The next four chapters consider some of the current practice in early childhood and provide reflections on emerging trends in program design. Fromberg examines the kindergarten curriculum from two perspectives, the academic-formal and the intellectual-experiential. She also deals with teacher certification and administrative practices. Caldwell offers a view of child care and education working hand in hand. Haskins and Alessi describe a successful model of racial integration and education in the Buffalo public school setting. Magid explores the benefits of employer-sponsored child care, with discussion of the probable consequences for young children, their families, and early childhood care providers.

The final four chapters illustrate and articulate the move of child care and early education specialists toward a more elaborated vision of the field. Bowman urges expansion and recognition of the personal experiential as well as the scientific bases for our knowledge and practice, while Rust and Kagan speak to the necessity of extending our awareness of the power we have to create and direct change in a rapidly shifting sociocultural milieu. Williams concludes with a discussion of future directions in the field, and their relation to ways early childhood specialists are choosing to express and enact their concerns—their professional language and actions.

This collection of essays is suggestive of more extensive changes to come in child care and early childhood education. It is a field still becoming. We look forward to the continuing, rapid evolution of this endeavor.

THE CARE AND EDUCATION
OF YOUNG CHILDREN

Expanding Contexts, Sharpening Focus

Welfare Reform: Serving America's Children

DANIEL PATRICK MOYNIHAN

United States Senate

Senator Moynihan restates the critical problems of family, children, and poverty in America that have been his driving concern for decades both as an academic and as a politician. He urges us to view welfare reform as the art of the possible and to develop policies that will save our children.

A quarter of a century has elapsed since Lyndon Johnson's initiative against poverty in America. About one American in six was poor in 1964. About one in six is poor today. In 1964, poverty was essentially a problem of the aged. In contrast, we look up today to find that not only are there more poor Americans than there were a quarter of a century ago, but that the poorest group in our population, one in five, are children (see Table 1).

This is a condition that has never before existed in our history.[1]

Table 1. Percentage below Poverty Level

Age group	1986
Under 18 years	19.8
18–64	11.1
65 and over	12.4

SOURCE: Current Population Reports, Consumer Income, Series P-60, No. 157, *Money, Income and Poverty Status of Families and Persons in the United States: 1986* (Advance data from the March 1987 Current Population Survey, U.S. Department of Commerce, Bureau of the Census).

How has this come about? At one level the answer is simple. It is, as Samuel H. Preston put it in the 1984 presidential address to the Population Association of America, "the earthquake that shuddered through the American family in the past 20 years"[2] — the twenty years, that is, from the beginning of the poverty program.

This is to say that a new dimension of poverty has emerged. As the 1986 census reported, nearly one in every four children (23.5 percent) lives with only one parent, two and one-third times the proportion in 1960 (see Table 2). The vast majority (89 percent) of these 14.8 million children live with their mothers. These include 18.3 percent of all white children, 53.1 percent of all black children, and 30.4 percent of all Hispanic children.

Table 2.   Children under 18 Living with One Parent
                     (Percent)

	1986	1960
Total	23.5	9.1
White	18.3	7.1
Black	53.1	21.9
Hispanic	30.4	(NA)

SOURCE: Current Population Reports, Population Characteristics, Series P-20, No. 418, *Marital Status and Living Arrangements: March, 1986* (U.S. Department of Commerce, Bureau of the Census), p. 8.

Estimates of the number of children who will live with a single parent at some point during childhood are yet more striking. Arthur Norton of the U.S. Bureau of the Census predicts that 61 percent of children born in 1987 will live for some time with only one biological parent before reaching the age of eighteen.[3] Inevitably, large numbers of these children will require some form of public assistance.

We do have programs to provide public assistance: Survivors' Insurance (SI) and Aid to Families with Dependent Children (AFDC). The Aid to Dependent Children (ADC) Program was created in 1935, as Title IV of the Social Security Act, to replace the widows' pension programs then operating in all but two states. Just as old age assistance was meant to serve as a temporary bridge until the Old Age Insurance Program matured, ADC was meant to tide over poor widows and orphans who were not yet entitled to receive the survivors' insurance benefits added to the Social Security Act in 1939.

In the 1930s, it was assumed that children lived in two-parent families, that one parent worked and the other kept house. It was further assumed that things would remain so. So long as and to the extent that the assumption was true, the transition from ADC to Survivors' Insurance worked smoothly. In 1986, a fully mature SI Program paid benefits to 3.3 million children. The program for dependent children, by now renamed Aid to Families with Dependent Children (AFDC), did not, however, wither away as expected. Rather it grew and grew as it was extended to single-parent families. The program now supports some 7 million children, twice the number of children receiving insured benefits under SI.

The characteristics of the populations served by these two programs are quite different. The majority of the children receiving SI are white. The majority of the children receiving AFDC are black or Hispanic (see Table 3).

Table 3.   Racial Composition of AFDC and Survivors' Insurance Caseloads
(Percent)

	SI	AFDC
White	66	40
Black	22	41
Hispanic	8	14
Other	4	5

SOURCE: Social Security Administration and Family Support Administration; AFDC data are for 1986; SI data are estimated for 1985.

The figures presented in Table 3 show that our public assistance programs seem to have created an extraordinary institutional bias against minority children. Since 1970, we have increased the real benefits received by children under SI by 53 percent. We have, in effect, cut the benefits of AFDC children by 13 percent by failing to index them to inflation. The federal government, the American people, now provide the average child receiving SI benefits almost three times what we provide a child on AFDC (see Table 4). The average provision for children under SI has been rising five times as fast as average family income since 1970, thus giving the lie to those who say we do not care about children. We do care about some children—majority children. It is minority children (not only but mostly) who are left behind.

Table 4.   Average Monthly AFDC and Survivors' Insurance Benefits Payments
(Per recipient payment, in constant 1986 dollars)

	SI	AFDC
1970	$222	$140
1986	339	122
Percent of change	+ 53	− 13

SOURCE: *Background Material and Data on Programs Within the Jurisdiction on the Committee on Ways and Means*, Committee on Ways and Means, U.S. House of Representatives, 100th Congress, 1st Session, 1987 edition, March 6, 1987. (*Note*: CRS put the numbers in current dollars. These do not appear in that form in the source book.)

This institutional bias extends to employment opportunities and economic-improvement options available to minority single-parent families.

Seventy-two percent of all mothers with children between the ages of six and eighteen are in the labor force. Over half of all mothers with children under the age of three are in the labor force. This marks a great change in the position of women in American life. The only women who have not participated in this change are the heads of AFDC families, of whom fewer than 5 percent work part time or full time.

How has this institutional bias against minority children and families emerged in our public assistance programs? I believe we know how. Welfare has become a stigmatized program, and the children dependent on it (as many as one child in three before reaching eighteen) are stigmatized by association. I believe we must get rid of that stigma by emphasizing child support, support to families, and the education and training adults need to get off welfare. Such a definition must occur at the federal level first. There has been a great deal of talk about both increasing child support and enabling adults through education and training, but the federal government has really never backed either. Once that stigma is gone, or diminished, states will once again feel the moral obligation to maintain and even increase AFDC payments to dependent children. The states are free to do so now. With but two exceptions, they do not. We must change this. AFDC should be a national program, with national benefits that keep pace with inflation, in exactly the same way that Survivors' Insurance is a national program with national benefits.

A child should never be neglected, even in a society brimming with children. How much more careful we ought to be then as children become a scarce resource. The U.S. birthrate dropped below the replacement level fifteen years ago. As a result, the number of young adults — age eighteen to twenty-four — as a percentage of the population will decline 23 percent by the year 2000. As this age group shrinks, there will be fewer adolescent mothers, fewer such mothers seeking public assistance and work training, and — perhaps most important — fewer young adults entering the labor force. The plain fact is that America has no children to waste. Yet, at present, we suffer the impoverishment of 20 percent of our children. Do we expect children growing up in misery to mature into adults capable of maintaining, much less improving, American society? Do we expect poor, ill-educated children to manage the American economy? It ought not to be left to chance.

Still, the conditions that have developed over a generation will not change overnight. It is possible, however, to change direction. We can and we must set a new trend in place by creating a new system of child support that, without abandoning ultimate security, puts its first emphasis on earned income, and that, without giving up on the problems of deeply dependent families, extends coverage to all needful ones. Welfare reform must become the art of the possible, or it will become a diversion of the essentially unserious.

Notes

1 New poverty data suggest this condition *has* existed in other nations. See Current Population Reports, Consumer Income, Series P-60, No. 157, *Money, Income and Poverty Status of Families and Persons in the United States: 1986* (Advance data from the March 1987 Current Population Survey, U.S. Department of Commerce, Bureau of the Census).

2 Samuel H. Preston, "Children and the Elderly: Divergent Paths for America's Dependents" (Presidential Address, Population Association of America, 1984).

3 Arthur Norton, Assistant Chief of Population Division, U.S. Bureau of the Census, Research Note, March 1987.

Economic Issues Related to Child Care and Early Childhood Education

MARIAN WRIGHT EDELMAN

Children's Defense Fund, Washington, D.C.

Seeing the economy and social structure of America as inexorably linked, Edelman explores the benefits of adequate child care to the family, the child, and the nation. She takes seriously the slogan, today's child is tomorrow's worker.

There are many false dichotomies in our perceptions of what constitutes public policy in the United States today. Nowhere is this more evident than in the way in which we assign separate categories to "social policy" and "economic policy" and fail to take into account the interrelationship and synergy between the two.

One glaring and critical example is our failure to recognize the connections between safe, affordable, quality child care and the barriers that prevent tens of thousands of Americans — present and future — from working to maximize the productivity of our society and our economy. The child of today is the worker of tomorrow. We say and hear this phrase over and over again — so often that we barely consider its implications. The opportunities available to a child help determine not only his or her eventual self-sufficiency or lack thereof, but also the degree to which that child becomes a productive adult who contributes to building the nation's economy.

The care and education of preschool children is an issue that has arrived fairly recently on the national policy agenda. Twenty years ago relatively few mothers of young children worked outside the home and quality child care was a luxury for a wealthy minority. Today, it is essential for the economic health and stability of millions of American families. This dramatic change has been stimulated by the inexorable march of mothers of young children into the work force, the increase in single-parent families, the decline in real wages of young families, and the recognition that too many of our children are growing up ill-equipped to succeed in the world economy, let alone to generate the level of income supports that will soon be needed by aging parents and grandparents.

Just what is this connection between the availability of day care and early childhood education and the future of the U.S. economy? By examining three key elements in the equation—the family, the individual, and the nation as a whole—we can arrive at some answers.

THE FAMILY

The most important factor in a child's healthy development is the existence of a nurturing, positive family environment. A family in which parents are losing the struggle to find work and to pay the rent and food bills may also be losing the fight for the healthy development of their children. Currently, economic uncertainty and poverty pose a constant threat to millions of American children. Particularly hard hit are the newly formed, young families with children who, despite the economic recovery of the 1980s, have actually lost economic ground compared with their peers in the 1970s. While real median family income for households headed by individuals forty-five to fifty-four rose 3 percent between 1973 and 1986, it actually declined more than 10 percent for families with a twenty-five to thirty-four-year-old head of household, and 24 percent for those with a household head under age twenty-five.[1]

Equally disturbing is the increasing incidence of births to unmarried, teenage mothers. Although total births to teen-agers have declined since 1970, the percentage of all teen births that are to unmarried teens rocketed from 13.9 in 1950 to 30 in 1970 to 58.7 in 1985.[2] Both these young mothers and their children face high risks of failure in the educational system and of living in poverty.

According to Census Bureau projections, the decade beginning in 1990 will mark a watershed in the demographic evolution of the American family:

> The 1990s will be the first decade to begin with a majority of mothers of young children (55 percent) in the work force, representing an increase of over 80 percent since 1970.

> The population of children under 10 from single-parent households will have risen from 6 million to 8.9 million—a 48 percent increase from the 1980s.

> The population of children under six will have increased 3.3 million to 23.0 million in 1990 (and will then begin to decline).[3]

In addition, the Department of Labor predicts that by 1995, more than 80 percent of women between the ages of twenty-four and forty-four will be in the work force. This compares with about half of the women in that age group in 1970.[4]

BUFFER AGAINST WELFARE DEPENDENCY AND POVERTY

For many of the still-growing population of single parents, child care is the only thing that stands between them and welfare dependency. If teen mothers, for example, do not have access to reliable and affordable child care, they are unlikely to return to high school or to find some other way of completing their education and prepare for the work force — a crucial step toward becoming independent and productive adults and avoiding additional pregnancies.

In a 1983 census bureau report on child-care arrangements among working mothers, single mothers cited difficulties with child-care arrangements as a major problem in seeking and keeping jobs. Forty-five percent of these women reported that they would be able to take a job if affordable child care were available.[5]

Similar results were reported in a study conducted by the General Accounting Office, which found that some 60 percent of respondents thought that lack of child care prevented their participation in work-training programs.[6] One of these parents, Annie Bridgers, a Washington, D.C., mother of three, told a congressional committee that access to subsidized day care enabled her to complete a job-training program, get off public assistance, and secure a job that generates income to support the family.[7] In the same hearing, another witness recounted: "Divorce took me from the upper middle class to complete poverty." With assistance from a social services program, she was able to enroll her young daughter in child care, attend college, and earn the bachelor's and law degrees that now make her a productive member of society.[8]

Such individual success stories are echoed in the collective experience of participants in initiatives such as Massachusetts's ET program, an employment, skills training, and education program including a substantial day-care component, that has placed over 30,000 welfare recipients in jobs since 1983.[9]

Experience shows that providing child care does make it possible for more parents to work to support their families and that making child care available to low-income working families costs less than maintaining them on welfare.[10] For many two-parent families, the second income, made possible by the availability of child care, is the only thing that stands between them and poverty.[11] Child care helps such families close the door on dependency and become economically self-sufficient in several ways: It enables them to replace welfare checks with salary checks and to stay on the job without the loss of work hours stemming from uncertain (or even dangerous), undependable, and discontinuous child-care arrangements; and it permits one or both adults in a family to work additional hours, thus increasing the family income.

HOW MUCH CHILD CARE AND FOR WHOM?

There is abundant evidence that lack of reliable, affordable child care is a major obstacle to parents' finding work, remaining employed, and increasing family income by working additional hours. More than a third of the women interviewed for a study reported in the *American Journal of Sociology* stated that they would like to work additional hours but are prevented from doing so by lack of available child care.[12] Research by University of Miami economists on the links between child care and economic self-sufficiency among low-income families living in public housing revealed that a 50 percent increase in the size of an on-site child-care center would result in a 13.5 percent rise in hours worked by residents and a 19.5 percent increase in their earnings.[13]

While availability and dependability of child-care services influence families' ability to use and benefit from them, an equally critical factor in access is cost. "Child care costs, the newest major expense for families, now consume nearly 10 percent of the average family's income and 20 percent of the income for poor families," noted Representative George Miller (D.-Calif.) in a congressional hearing.[14] This increase in the proportion of income needed for child care is occurring at a time when the average income for young families with children has declined and other costs, such as paying for housing, are increasing.

Because of the cost factor, the families whose youngsters most need child care are the least able to afford it. In 1985, fewer than one-third of four-year-olds and 17 percent of three-year-olds in families with incomes below $10,000 a year were enrolled in preschool programs. In that same year, however, 67 percent of four-year-olds and 54 percent of three-year-olds whose families had incomes of $35,000 a year or more attended preschool programs.[15]

If poor families do figure out a way to pay for child care from their low or sporadic incomes, all too often the care they can afford may be in an unsafe or inadequately staffed facility, such as a neighbor's home. Few are able to afford the cost of developmentally enriching child-care programs that would increase the chances of poor and at-risk children to overcome the health, environmental, and other disadvantages that accompany poverty. Currently, the highly successful, federally supported Head Start Program serves less than 20 percent of eligible children.[16]

This brings us to the second element of the equation: the relationship of child care and early childhood experience to the child's future role and competence in society and in the economy.

THE CHILD

Just as the availability of safe, affordable child care is linked to the ability of low-income parents to move from dependency to self-sufficiency, there is also linkage between quality child care and preschool programs and the nation's future.

At the most basic level, a child requires protection from a health- or life-threatening environment. The sad litany of accidents and other tragedies such as burning to death in a clothes dryer, drowning in a well, or being caught in a home fire that have taken the lives of children in inadequate care (or at home alone because of lack of access to care) will continue to unfold until we commit ourselves to providing safe, adequate care for all who need it. Our vision for our children must, however, go far beyond mere physical survival.

The first high school graduating class of the twenty-first century entered first grade in September 1988. These preschoolers are future leaders, workers, parents, college students, taxpayers, soldiers, and the hope of the twenty-first century. Many of them and their young siblings are off to a healthy start, but millions are not:

One in four of these children is poor.

One in three is nonwhite, of whom two in five are poor.

One in five is at risk of becoming a teen parent.

One in six is in a family in which neither parent has a job.

One in seven is at risk of dropping out of school.[17]

For these children and those that will follow them, access to quality child-care services may determine not only their prospects for success in school, but their prospects for success in life, for example, the risk of falling prey to dependency, handicapping conditions, psychological problems, and even crime.

LONG-TERM EFFECTS

Success in school depends on a foundation of psychological development and social skills as well as on intellectual factors. Researchers and others have found that youngsters who lack access to quality child care may arrive at school ill-prepared to succeed. Two decades of experience with Head Start and other quality early childhood programs, however, show that poor and other at-risk youngsters can be helped by such programs to overcome their disadvantages and become successful in school, work, and social roles. Among the education-related benefits cited for children who attend preschool compared with those who do not are the following:

Better grades, fewer failing marks, fewer retentions in grade, and fewer absences in elementary school.

Less need of special education services and fewer placements in special education classes.

Improved literacy and curiosity in school.

Greater likelihood of completing high school and of continuing education beyond high school.[18]

Examples abound. Participants in South Carolina's half-day child-development program for four-year-olds arrived in school better prepared to learn to read than those who did not have the experience. Participants in Syracuse, New York's early education program were studied ten years later and found to have higher academic achievement and less school absence than peers who did not participate. The Perry Preschool Program in Michigan was found to have "increased the percentage of persons who were literate, employed, and enrolled in postsecondary education, whereas it . . . reduced the percentages who were school dropouts, labelled mentally retarded, on welfare or arrested for delinquent and criminal activity."[19] In sum, the effects of quality child care and preschool education endure long beyond a child's entry into kindergarten or first grade.

At the same time, it is important to realize that the need for child care does not end when a child goes to kindergarten or first grade. The importance of providing after-school care was exhibited dramatically when the editors of *Spring*, a magazine for fourth, fifth, and sixth graders, asked their readers to write to them about a situation they found "scary." The editors were stunned to discover that nearly 70 percent of the seven thousand letters that poured in dealt with fear of being home alone, most while parents were working.[20] In interviews with more than one thousand teachers, the Metropolitan Life Insurance Company found that the majority cited isolation and lack of supervision after school as the major reason children have difficulty in school.[21]

THE NATION

In 1978, young people between the ages of sixteen and twenty-four made up 27 percent of the working-age population, but, by 1995, they will account for only 18 percent.[22] The rapid decline in the percentage of young people and children in the population makes its essential that we devise ways to maximize the competence of our future work force. As this demographic trend plays itself out, the value of each individual young worker to business and industry increases.

Research is beginning to demonstrate what common sense had told us for many years. In addition to the social benefits of high-quality child care, such as less delinquency and fewer dropouts, there are also measurable economic benefits:

> The value of benefits to participants and to the nation far exceeds the initial cost of the program. In the case of the Perry Project, it is estimated that a $1 investment in preschool education returns $6 in taxpayer savings because of lower education costs, lower costs of public welfare and crime, and higher worker productivity.[23]

> The "head start" afforded by quality child care or preschool enhances a child's prospects of being employable as an adult, and of earning more (and paying more taxes) than he or she would have without the strong

foundation built in the early years.[24]

Employers are more likely to be spared the cost and difficulties associated with hiring workers who lack basic skills and of training or retraining them.[25]

Employers and the economy benefit from quality, dependable child care since the working parents who use the child-care services are more productive on the job.[26]

A *Fortune* magazine survey of 405 employed parents in dual-earner families identified several ways in which lack of child care detracts from the ability of parents to carry out their work effectively. For parents who lacked child care, the absence of such service was one of the most significant predictors of job absenteeism. In addition, parents who had access to some child care but had to contend with breakdowns in the system were more likely to arrive at work late, leave early, and exhibit stress-related symptoms, all of which undermine their effectiveness on the job.[27]

Employers who have provided child-care services or assisted employees to find them think that they have been rewarded. Harry L. Freeman of the American Express Company describes the benefits of employer-sponsored child care in this way: "When employees know their children are in good hands, tardiness and absenteeism are lower . . . recruitment and retention are easier . . . morale and self-esteem are better . . . and productivity is higher."[28]

The experience of American Express is not unique. Between 1983 and 1987, the number of employers providing some type of child care assistance to their employees increased 400 percent.[29] Assistance ranges from sponsoring seminars on parenting, to helping employees find child care, to increasing the supply of family day-care centers, to sponsoring on-site centers. Few employers, however, offer a full-scale program or actually help their employees pay for child care. Of those that do, the form of assistance most often provided is a "salary reduction plan" in which up to $5,000 in child-care expenses may be deducted from the employee's salary, thus reducing his or her tax liability. This system, obviously, tends to benefit more highly paid employees.

Despite the increase in the number and variety of employer-sponsored child-care services, they are the least frequently offered of all employee benefits. It is estimated that only three thousand of the nation's six million employers offer some type of child-care service; the majority of employers that offer on-site child care are hospitals, using the service as an incentive for recruiting nurses. Expenditures for early education in the 1985–1986 school year were $1.5 million — a tiny fraction of the $140 billion spent on education preschool through secondary.[30] Thus, despite some progress, child-care assistance appears to remain a low priority in both government and industry.

THE PUBLIC ROLE

In the twenty years since we began debating the value of early childhood programs, the chorus of voices calling for a commitment to quality care has expanded to include representatives of many segments of our society, from parents and social-program advocates to economic and business leaders, to religious organizations and public officials. This chorus of voices representing so many disparate segments of our society is sending a clear message that our increasing need for child care and early education can be met only through a partnership of the federal government, state and local governments, and the private sector.

In recent years, business and government have endorsed the concept of "early investment" in children, a concept that places child care and education of youth at the heart of the country's future economic well-being and involves government, education, and industry in partnership to sponsor educational improvement. The nation's governors espoused this viewpoint in their 1986 report *Time for Results*.[31] The concept is articulated by the Committee for Economic Development, a group of 225 corporate officers and university presidents, in the introduction to *Children in Need:* "This nation cannot continue to compete and prosper in the global arena when more than one fifth of our children live in poverty and a third grow up in ignorance. And if the nation cannot compete, it cannot lead."[32] In 1988, more than 130 national organizations united to form the Alliance for Better Child Care to work for congressional passage of the Act for Better Child Care (S. 1885, H. 3660), a measure that will help provide safe, affordable, quality child care for the low-income families who so desperately need it.

As the 1980s draw to a close, we are struggling to increase productivity and restore our competitiveness in world markets. We are experiencing the pain that comes from being bested by nations that have placed a higher priority on preparing all of their children for productive roles in the national economy. We must act now to reverse the effects of the trends that are crippling our future work force at an early age. A commitment to providing early childhood education is more than a logical extension of the commitment we already make to children from five to eighteen, and to college students. It is a national imperative. As the population of youth declines, every one of our children becomes more precious to us, not just to our families but to our economy.

Until we as a nation commit ourselves to starting at the beginning, we will always be playing catch-up. Our business leaders know this. Many of our political leaders are saying it. Now it is time to do something about it. Our nation cannot afford, morally or economically, to continue to waste this most precious of resources.

Notes

1   *Children's Defense Budget, FY 1989* (Washington, D.C.: Children's Defense Fund, 1988), p. 85.

2   *Teenage Pregnancy: An Advocate's Guide to the Numbers* (Washington, D.C.: Adolescent Pregnancy Prevention Clearinghouse, Children's Defense Fund, January/March 1988), p. 11.

3   U.S. Department of Commerce, Bureau of Census, *Current Population Reports*, Series P-25, No. 952, "Projections of the Population of the United States by Age, Sex, and Race: 1983 to 2080" (May 1984), Table 6, Middle Series.

4   "American Families in Tomorrow's Economy" (Hearing before the Select Committee on Children, Youth, and Families, U.S. House of Representatives, July 1, 1987), p. 11.

5   U.S. Bureau of Census, *Current Population Reports*, Series P-23, No. 129, "Child-Care Arrangements of Working Mothers, June 1982" (Washington, D.C.: U.S. Government Printing Office, 1983), Table H.

6   U.S. General Accounting Office, *Work and Welfare: Current AFDC Work Programs and Implications for Federal Policy*, GAO/HRD 87–34 (Washington, D.C., January 1987), p. 86.

7   "Child Care: Key to Employment in a Changing Economy," Hearing before the Select Committee on Children, Youth, and Families (Washington, D.C.: U.S. House of Representatives, March 10, 1987), p. 8.

8   Ibid., p. 9.

9   Ibid., p. 17.

10   *Children's Defense Budget*, p. 178. As an example of the extent of the savings involved, the State of Colorado found that it costs 38 percent less to provide day care for working parents than to maintain the same families on the public assistance and Medicaid benefits they would require if unemployed.

11   Sheldon Danziger and Peter Gottshalk, "How Have Families with Children Been Faring?" (Presentation to the Joint Economic Committee, Washington, D.C., November 1985). The committee found that the 1984 earnings for two-parent families were 23.4 percent higher than they would have been had wives not worked.

12   Harriet Presser and Wendy Baldwin, "Child Care as a Constraint in Employment: Prevalence Correlates Being on the Work and Fertility Nexus," *The American Journal of Sociology* 85 (1980): 5.

13   "Child Care: Key to Employment in a Changing Economy," p. 149.

14   "American Families in Tomorrow's Economy," p. 1. Note: The cost of child care now averages over $3,000 per year, and infant care often costs $100 per week per child.

15   *State Child Care Fact Book* (Washington, D.C.: Children's Defense Fund, 1987), p. 24. From data supplied to the U.S. Department of Education Center for Educational Statistics by researchers Sheila Kamerman and Alfred Kahn of Columbia University.

16   *Project Head Start Statistical Fact Sheet*, Fiscal Year 1988 (Washington, D.C.: Administration for Children, Youth, and Families, Office of Human Services, Department of Health and Human Services).

17   *Child Care: The Time Is Now* (Washington, D.C.: Children's Defense Fund, 1987), p. 6.

18   "Opportunities for Success: Cost-Effective Programs for Children, Update 1988" (Hearing before the Select Committee on Children, Youth, and Families) (Washington, D.C.: U.S. House of Representatives, 1988), p. 39.

19   Ibid., p. 40.

20   As cited by Dale B. Fink in "Latch Key Children and School Age Child Care," Background briefing prepared for the Appalachian Educational Laboratory School Age Child Care Project (Wellesley, Mass.: Wellesley College Center for Research on Women, 1986), p. 4.

21   Louis Harris and Associates, "Strengthening the Links between Home and School" (Survey of the American Teacher sponsored by the Metropolitan Life Insurance Company, 1987).

22   Ellen Galinsky, Testimony before the Subcomittee on Children, Families, Drugs and Alcoholism, U.S. Senate, March 15, 1988, p. 11.

23   J. R. Berreuter-Clement et al., *Changed Lives: The Effects of the Perry School Program on Youths through Age 19* (Ypsilanti, Mich.: Monographs of the High/Scope Educational Research Foundation, 8, 1984), p. 90.

24   Ibid., p. 88.

25   Ibid.

26   "Child Care: Key to Employment in a Changing Economy," p. 56. This survey of 405 employed parents in dual-earner families suggests that this benefit accrues to employers of workers at all income levels, not just those living on the economic margin.

27   Ibid., p. 4.

28   Ibid., p. 56.

29   *State Child Care Fact Book*, p. 27.

30   "Child Care: Key to Employment in a Changing Economy," p. 217.

31   *Time for Results: Task Force on Readiness* (Washington, D.C.: National Governors' Association Center for Policy Research and Analysis, August 1986).

32   *Children in Need: Investment Strategies for the Educationally Disadvantaged* (New York: Committee for Economic Development, 1987), p. 1.

Racism and the Education
of Young Children

JAMES P. COMER
Yale University

In the child's development, when and how does the concept of race arise? How can primary and secondary caregivers help a child in a racist society develop a positive self-image and achieve a healthy understanding of racial and cultural diversity?

A four-year-old black child slapped her doll and said, "Shut up, you black bitch!" Her white teacher, horrified and confused by the incident, retreated without a response. In a second situation, several white classmates of a black child spoke to her in racially derogatory ways. Her mother complained to her teacher and to the principal. They both acknowledged the incidents but indicated that the children intended no harm. The principal did eventually agree to move the child to the classroom of a second white teacher at the same grade level. Several days later the child sent her mother a card on which she had drawn a big red heart with a note that read: "Thank you, Mommy, my teacher touched me [an affectionate hug] today."

In the first case, the child and her family were victims of long-standing societal racism that had been institutionalized and internalized, and was being prepared for transmission to the next generation. Because the pervasiveness and multiple manifestations of racism have not been acknowledged, nor adequately addressed, the teacher was not in a position to help minimize its harmful effects. In the second situation, overt racism was acceptable, harmful, but limited in the case of this particular child largely because of the action of her mother. Because of racism and its pervasiveness, however, its victims are unable, disproportionately, to limit its effects and ancillary problems.

Racism interferes with the normal development of those children subjected to it. It hampers their ability to function at their full potential as children and, later, as adults. This contributes to their greater involvement in social problems such as poor school learning, juvenile delinquency, teenage pregnancy, and substance abuse. These problems decrease our human resources, drain our financial resources, and intensify intergroup relationship problems. They permit and promote harmful assumptions that, in turn, interfere with the development and functioning of majority-group children, adults, and institutions.

It is estimated that by the early 1990s minorities will make up one-third of our work force.[1] Unless minority children are fully prepared to participate in the job market of tomorrow, the economy will be adversely affected. Unless minority and majority children are prepared to function adequately in an open society, our quality of life will be lowered and our democratic ideals will never be realized. Once racist attitudes, values, and ways are established in individuals, change is difficult. Thus, prevention in early childhood is extremely important, yet early childhood education has not given adequate attention to this matter.

In this article, I will discuss the ways that racism affects child development. Then, I will briefly discuss the historic racial experiences and reaction to them that have made it difficult for us to address racism. Third, I will discuss the implications of racism and its history in this country for the preparation and practice of early childhood professionals.

RACISM AND CHILD DEVELOPMENT

Because of the dependent nature of the child, the parent or caretaker must provide for essential needs. In the process, the relationship needs of child and caretaker are met and lead to an emotional attachment or bond between them. This enables the caretaker to influence the development of the child along multiple growth pathways, five of which are critical to school learning: social-interactive, psycho-emotional, moral, speech-language, and cognitive-intellectual-academic. Interactions between parent and child in almost every setting—from a bedtime story to discussing safety precautions, or a trip to the grocery store—provide the content and context for growth and development.

The child needs the guidance, protection, and approval—and resulting security—the caretaker provides. This need motivates the child to behave more often than not in an adult-satisfying manner. A cycle of generally acceptable performance and approval is set in motion. Approval gives the young child a sense of acceptance and belonging and a related sense of well-being. Disapproval, rejection, and neglect are sources of anxiety.

The parents are the first members of the larger society in the life of the child. They are members of a social network that may or may not be a part of the social mainstream. They bring their particular skills and the social network attitudes, values, and ways to the task of child care and rearing. Because of the extreme dependency of the child and the important role of the caretaker, the attitudes, values, and ways of the caretaker greatly influence those of the young child. This allows the caretaker to mediate the child's experiences — to give them meaning and to establish their relative importance.

Also, the psychosocial status of the child is derived from that of the parent. The education, economic condition, religion, and belief system of the parents all affect the quality of care the child receives from them. The social status and race of the parent often affect the expectations of the child by parents and others alike. When the child enters a larger network of social contacts, his or her behavior and skills elicit a positive or negative reaction. Frequent success and approval deepens and enlarges a child's previously gained sense of well-being and confidence. A positive sense of self begins to emerge, but it is highly vulnerable. Adults must be able to protect the young child from experiences that undermine his or her sense of well-being, adequacy, and confidence.

Cognitive development around three years of age permits a child to become aware of racial difference and it is here that he or she can first directly experience the effects of racism. It is here that caretakers should be able to help children feel positive about their own racial group and that of others. Positive feelings about race can enlarge a child's overall desirable sense of self. Negative feelings about race can plant seeds of self-doubt even among children who are developing well otherwise.[2]

There is a more subtle and serious problem for many minority children. Race-related social conditions, past and present, have put a disproportionate number of minority parents under stress. Many are not able to provide their children with the kind of developmental experiences that will prepare them for school or elicit positive responses from others. Some are underdeveloped along critical developmental pathways. Some display attitudes, values, and ways that are different from those of the mainstream.[3] This was the case for the four-year-old who slapped her doll in the vignette above. Such behaviors are sometimes believed to be due to the race of the child. Even when this is not the case, caretakers — for reasons described below — are often not able to respond appropriately. Negative racial feelings and behaviors are maintained. The child's behavior reinforces adverse expectations and behaviors of even the most empathetic caretaker. Reactions from guilt through avoidance to pity and permissiveness are as harmful as overt racial antagonism.

Majority children, and more fortunate minority children, interacting with minority children from families under stress often gain racial perceptions that are harmful to themselves and to minorities. For example, two six-year-old first graders — one black, one white, and both from middle-income families — were walking to school. They encountered a group of black children from a housing project who attended the same school. The white child said to her black friend, "Hold my hand, here come the black kids, and they fight." From her point of view, her black friend was not "black." Such perceptions are harmful to all involved.

Adequately functioning minority parents usually help their children understand such perceptions, and show them that the problem or shortcoming is with the person who displays misperceptions or outright racial antagonisms, not in themselves. Such parents usually teach their children to manage overt racial antagonisms in ways that minimize the frequency of such attacks, and their psychosocial damage. When minority parents are comfortable with their own racial identity, their children have a good chance of acquiring the same level of comfort. They acquire their racial and ethnic culture from their parents and the experiences they expose them to in a natural and positive way. For many, however, this is not the case. Often, as in the case above, child-care workers are not able to protect children from the negative effects of racism, even when they would like to do so. As in the second case above, the caretakers—teachers and principals—are sometimes the source of the racist attitudes, or make no effort to protect the black child. Again, many black parents are victims of racism to the point that they cannot protect their children from its negative effects.

The effects of racism begin to impact children more directly after eight or nine years of age. Somewhere between eight and twelve children begin to "place" themselves and their families in the social status structure that they have begun to observe. They begin to internalize the attitudes about themselves held by powerful individuals in their environment—parents, teachers, others—and they often act on or react to these expectations in a self-fulfilling manner. School curricula, television programs, people and practices, regularly convey messages about race that can be troublesome to minority children.

Many minority children have no way to understand the inequities in the society as anything but deficits within their own group. This can be troublesome even for black young people who are developing reasonably well overall, creating outright racial identity problems for many during adolescence. Without a mechanism to counter the negative messages about themselves transmitted in the larger society, some associate problem behavior with their minority identity. Among some, school achievement or high-level aspirations become nonminority activities. Some successful minority young people who are uncomfortable with their identity attempt to distance themselves from their group. For example, the first black valedictorian at a suburban high school in Ohio said, "I'm tired of hearing all this stuff about being the first black; I'm an individual and that's the only thing that counts." Such attitudes and behaviors among the most able minority students limit the peer support available to undermine the effects of racism in this country, and in turn permit racism to interfere with the development of black children in the next generation.

HISTORY, RACISM, AND CHILD DEVELOPMENT

We have reacted to our historical racial experience in ways that make it extremely difficult to overcome its contemporary adverse effects on child development. Many Americans—black and white—would prefer to end past race-based inequities and injustices and try to create a more just society without fully considering the effects of the past. We are embarrassed, guilty, and ashamed of the treatment of blacks, Native Americans, and Hispanics in particular. Many see no political, economic, or social benefit for themselves in fully considering the adverse effects of the past on these groups. Because our society has avoided, denied, and rationalized the more difficult and more troublesome outcomes of our historical racial experience on these groups, we have facilitated race-based public policy and practices that victimize these groups even more.

The textbooks and curricula in most schools inadequately address our racial history. Some do not address it at all. Schools of higher education are only slightly better. Even the social and behavioral sciences and social services give inadequate attention to historical public policy and social context issues that focus more on the affected groups and individuals. Most relevant here, many schools of education give little attention to the way in which minority students have been disadvantaged, and what to do about it. As a result, some of the most educated people in America—policymakers and trend setters—do not have the knowledge base necessary to understand and address race-based problems. Thus, it is not uncommon to hear even well-meaning people say, "We [their ethnic group] made it, why can't the blacks—or browns?"

Without an understanding of the fundamental difference between the European and Asian immigrant experience and that of blacks, we cannot understand and interpret the forces of racism in the society in general, and in early childhood education in particular. Racism's most serious damage was done by disrupting the organizing aspects of the culture of victimized groups.[4] This resulted in adverse effects on institutional life, particularly family life, and in turn on child development. I will briefly review the European and Asian experience in this regard, and while the underlying problem is the same for other minority groups, I will confine my discussion in this paper to the experience of blacks.

All immigrant groups experienced hardship, but most also experienced a reasonable degree of continuity. They were able to continue their religion, language, and other aspects of their culture in the new country. Many came in groups, voluntarily, from the old country and settled together in the new country. These circumstances often created a fair degree of cohesion within immigrant groups.[5]

Most immigrants were able to vote within a short period of time. This facilitated the acquisition of political power in one generation and, in turn, brought economic and social power. Usually a few members of a group either brought or had access to wealth from the old country. Political, economic, and social power within the mainstream of the society created networks of contacts, ties, and information that first served to decrease the antagonism toward their group, and then to pull many other families into networks of mainstream opportunity. These developments made education available and important. As a result, immigrants were able to undergo in three generations development that paralleled economic development in this country. Our most massive immigration occurred before 1915. Before 1900 it was possible to earn a living without an education and to create the level of family stability that would enable children to participate in a job market between 1900 and 1945 that required a moderate level of education and training. Families able to participate in the job market of this period were in the best position to enable their children to acquire the high level of education and skills necessary to participate in the economy between 1945 and 1980, and so on into the postindustrial economy after 1980. While there were psychosocial casualties due to the dislocation and hardships related to immigration, there were fewer among these immigrant groups than among groups that experienced more traumatic social histories.

The black beginnings — as Americans — were marked by cultural discontinuity, rather than continuity. Blacks experienced the loss of their organizing institutions — political, economic, and social. In West Africa, these institutions were providing adaptive attitudes, values, and ways. The culture of slavery that was imposed broke this influence. Slavery was a system of forced dependency and inherent inferiority, without hope of a better future. Slave parents were not preparing their children for a prideful place or greater opportunity in the new culture. These conditions produced severely negative psychosocial consequences for many. Some made adaptive responses that protected them from the most adverse effects of slavery, and some lived under less harsh conditions of slavery. A black church was created out of the aesthetic remnants of African culture and the Protestant religion of slavemasters.[6] Some slaves were able to identify with the best aspects of their masters and the new culture. Even these adaptations, however, left the slaves vulnerable to negative identifications as a racial group. In fact, they were not a single and cohesive ethnic group. All of these conditions made cultural cohesion during and after slavery extremely difficult.

After slavery, violence and subterfuge were used to deny most blacks the vote.[7] As a result, blacks were closed out of mainstream political, economic, and social power. They had no access to wealth. Without power, the group could not decrease the high level of racism and the denial of opportunity. As a result, in the eight states that had 80 percent of the black population right into the 1930s, educational expenditures for white children were four to eight times those for black children. In some places the disparity was as great as twenty-five times or more.[8] The same disparity existed in higher education. As late as the mid-1960s, the combined endowment of two prestigious white women's colleges was equal to one-half that of a single Ivy League college serving white males; and the one-half endowment of the latter was greater than that of the more than one hundred black colleges put together.[9]

Even educated black people were closed out of the economic mainstream. In order to facilitate segregation, a black leadership group, serving blacks, was allowed to emerge in religion and the professional areas only. These conditions denied blacks the contacts, knowledge, and experiences of mainstream political, economic, and social institutions, and the ability to pull families into them, or to make education possible and meaningful to the widest number of people. Despite this, the supportive and adaptive nature of rural culture and the black church enabled many families to do reasonably well until the 1950s. As late as the 1940s, only slightly over 20 percent of all black families were single-parent families; now the statistic is around 50 percent. Most black communities were reasonably safe through the 1950s.[10] Around 1945, however, education became the ticket for admission to living-wage jobs. Blacks, closed out of the educational mainstream during the period when most Americans were gaining the education needed to participate in the last stage of the industrial era and beyond, were most hurt.

Exclusion from the primary job market, combined with urbanization and the significant decline of black church influence, put a large number of families under great stress. Many families that once functioned well began to function less well in urban areas north and south. After 1945, well-functioning families from all groups began to have fewer children, except where there were religious reasons. This was not the case for poorly functioning families, of whom, for historic reasons, a disproportionate number were black.

Because of racist policies, practices, and structural changes, blacks were not able to undergo the same degree of the three-generational movement as other groups. Nonetheless, there were three generations of development among many black families. It is this group that has been able to take advantage of opportunities created by the elimination of the legal structures supporting racism. Those families most victimized by past conditions of racism and structural changes are least able to take advantage of new opportunities. These constitute the group that American institutions have not brought into the mainstream of society.

American institutions made an inadequate adjustment to structural changes after World War II. We did not develop the kinds of housing, health, and educational policies that could have interrupted the residual effects of racism and related poverty, that could have reduced the stress on black families. Today, many families under stress are unable to give their children the kinds of experiences that can prepare them to succeed in school and in life. Even many functioning reasonably well are excluded from the mainstream of the society to the point that they often do not know how to provide their children with experiences that can enable them to succeed.

The black community has been preoccupied with trying to reduce racism without having access to the traditional mainstream power base. It has not had the cohesion and power needed to positively affect the lives of its most victimized families. As a result, too many underachieve, and behave in troublesome ways. Racism allowed many to accept the academic under-achievement and troublesome behavior of many children from the most vic-timized black families as evidence of their lack of ability and undesirability, rather than as consequences of exclusion from the societal mainstream. This has resulted in school failure and other social problems rather than the social mainstream success that was, and is, possible for most Americans.

The black experience described above permits a black child to slap her doll and say, "Shut up you black bitch"; permits some white school personnel to ignore racist intimidation of black children, or to participate in it; permits black children to experience conditions and pick up information that contrib-utes to negative racial identities; permits white children to make inaccurate assumptions about blacks, and their own racial group; and, finally, permits our institutions, even those preparing teachers to help children grow and learn, to ignore the past effects of racism to the point that they cannot help children avoid the adverse consequences of it.

IMPLICATIONS FOR EARLY CHILDHOOD EDUCATION:
TRAINING AND PRACTICE

In 1968 our Yale Child Study Center team — a psychiatrist, a social worker, a special education teacher, and a psychologist — went into two inner-city schools that were troublesome expressions of our nation's racial policy. The students were 99 percent black, and almost all were poor. In 1969, the achievement level of the fourth graders in these schools was thirty-second and thirty-third out of thirty-three schools. These students were nineteen and eighteen months behind in language arts and mathematics. We termi-nated the program in one school after five years because both staff and par-ents there were comfortable with the changes that had been made and were unwilling to proceed further. We entered a second school with a similar pro-file to that of the school we had been serving. The majority of students in the new school were also drawn from a housing project. By 1984, the two schools, without any changes in socioeconomic makeup, were tied for the third and fourth highest level achievement on the IOWA Test of Basic Skills. One school was a year above, and the second was seven months above grade level. Attendance and behavior in these schools were among the best in the city. These outcomes were achieved by using our knowledge of history, child development, and human-system interactions to understand the behavior of parents, staff, and students in school. With this understanding, we were able to create mechanisms, programs, and practices in the school that overcame those effects of racism and poverty that limited the school performance of staff and students, and school support among parents.

A major task was to overcome partially race-based assumptions among staff and parents about the ability and troublesome behavior of the students. Through an understanding of the historical experience of blacks, the staff came to appreciate how many of the students were prepared for life in the nonmainstream social network of their families, but were not prepared for the mainstream experience and expectations of the school. This led to a project entitled "The Social Skills Curriculum for Inner City Children." This curriculum involved parents and integrated the teaching of basic skills, social skills, and appreciation of the arts. It included an appreciation of black culture. This program facilitated positive home-school relationships, greater student growth and development, and a positive racial identity among the students. It also resulted in significantly improved achievement and social behavior.

None of the teachers had had the kind of preservice training that would have enabled them to work in the ways needed with the children, parents, and each other. In-service activities had to be provided. This should not have been necessary in a multicultural society committed to providing children from all socioeconomic backgrounds with the kind of education that allows them to achieve at the level of their ability. Preservice programs — in and outside the discipline of education — should provide all students with an understanding of how structural forces, policies, and practices impact communities, groups and families, and child development.

Race has been a central issue in American life. The ways in which it has affected child development must be considered in preservice programs. Teachers should have an opportunity — both in pre- and in-service training — to learn the ways in which their behavior can either facilitate or interfere with the development of children. They should be prepared to address the race-related needs of minority children. Because of the power of early childhood educators to influence child development, it is critically important that their educational training provide them with the knowledge, skills, and sensitivity to protect children from racial attitudes and conditions that interfere with development. Early childhood educators must be prepared to promote the development and learning of children who are attempting to grow and learn in spite of race-based obstacles to their success.

Notes

1   "Here They Come, Ready or Not," *Education Week,* Special Report, May 14, 1986, p. 31.

2   James P. Comer and Alvin F. Poussant, *Black Child Care* (New York: Simon & Schuster, 1975).

3   James P. Comer, *School Power: Implications of an Intervention Project* (New York: Free Press, 1980).

4   James P. Comer, *Beyond Black and White* (New York: Quadrangle/New York Times Books, 1972).

5   Marcus Lee Hansen, *The Immigrant in American History* (Cambridge: Harvard University Press, 1940).

6   E. Franklin Frazier, *The Negro Church in America* (New York: Schocken Books, 1963).

7   John Hope Franklin, *Reconstruction after the Civil War* (Chicago: University of Chicago Press, 1961).

8   David T. Blose and Ambrose Caliver, *Statistics on the Education of Negroes, 1929–1932,* Bulletin #13, U.S. Office of Education (Washington, D.C.: Department of the Interior, 1936).

9   Council for Financial Aid to Education, *1964–65 Voluntary Support of America's Colleges and Universities* (New York: Council for Financial Aid to Education, 1967).

10   U.S. Bureau of the Census, *Statistical Abstract of the United States* (Washington, D.C.: U.S. Department of Commerce, 1951 and 1987).

Early Interventions to Reduce Intergenerational Disadvantage: The New Policy Context

LISBETH B. SCHORR

Harvard University Medical School

Schorr considers the complex array of factors that put young children at risk. She cites numerous successful programs that have already demonstrated their potency and argues that we can deal with the large-scale problems of disadvantage only if we are willing to mount equally large-scale interventions.

The environment in which new policies and programs for the care and education of young children will develop has recently undergone such rapid change as to require a fresh assessment of where we now stand.

The new context is the product, first, of changed public perceptions about society's stake in investing in children and, second, vastly increased knowledge about the nature of effective programs.

SOCIETY'S STAKE

Investment in improved services to young children, especially poor children, is increasingly recognized as essential to the welfare of every American.[1] Connections have been documented between early interventions and later outcomes such as the incidence of welfare dependence, crime, school-age pregnancy, and school dropout (see Table 1). A public concerned about the high numbers of young people leaving school without the skills and motivation to work, about weakening productivity, losses in international competitiveness, growing costs of prisons and welfare, and the prospect of a permanent American underclass is becoming ever more receptive to evidence that effective early interventions[2] have long-term payoffs. Economic, technological, and demographic trends that have resulted in more mothers working, fewer young people available for entry-level jobs, and a rise in the level of skill needed for employment have added to the general sense that current policies that govern the nation's investment in human capital and impact on

Table 1.   Examples of Quantified Effects of Selected Interventions

Intervention	*Outcome*		
School-based health clinic, St. Paul, Minn. St. Paul-Ramsey County Medical Center 1973–present	Childbearing among female students in first two participating high schools decreased by more than 50 percent within three years		
School-related health clinic, Baltimore, Md., serving junior and senior high school with all-black, low-income student bodies totaling over 1,700 students Johns Hopkins University School of Medicine 1982–1984	Among 695 female respondents (of whom about three-fourths were sexually active), the proportion of sexually active ninth to twelfth grade girls who became pregnant declined by 25 percent; the rate in comparison school went up 58 percent in same period		

Augmented, comprehensive prenatal care for 7,000 low-income women in thirteen California counties
 	
California State Department of Health
 	
1979–1982
	LBW (<2500 gm) rate
	    among participants:
	    among comparison group:
	
	VLBW (<1500 gm) rate
	    among participants:
	    among comparison group:
		4.7%
		7.0%
		
		0.5%
		1.3%	

Augmented, comprehensive prenatal care for 744 school-aged pregnant girls, mostly black and single, all poor, Baltimore, Md.
 	
Johns Hopkins University
School of Medicine
 	
1979–1981
	LBW (<2500 gm) rate
	    among participants:
	    among comparison group:
	
	VLBW (<1500 gm) rate
	    among participants:
	    among comparison group:
		9.9%
		16.4%
		
		1.9%
		3.9%	

Home visiting to 305 pregnant teenagers by lay "Resource Mothers" in rural South Carolina
 	
South Carolina State Health Department
 	
1981–1983
	LBW (<2500 gm) rate
	    among participants:
	    among random controls:
	
	VLBW (<1500 gm) rate
	    among participants:
	    among random controls:
		10%
		13%
		
		1%
		4.5%	

Homebuilders intensive in-home crisis and family-preservation services, Tacoma and Seattle, Wash. Catholic Children's Services and Homebuilders 1974–present; evaluation 1983–1985	In 88% of families in which removal of child was imminent when intervention began, family was intact and child had not been removed one year later		

Comprehensive health, child care, and social services for 18 infants aged 0–2½ and their families, New Haven, Conn.
 	
Yale University Child Study Center
 	
1968–1972
	At 10 year follow-up:
	
	Average years of education completed by mother:
	    participants:
	    comparison:
		13.0
		11.7	

Table 1.   Examples of Quantified Effects of Selected Interventions (Continued)

Intervention	*Outcome*
	Average number of children in family: participants: 1.67 comparison: 2.2
	Proportion of families self-supporting: participants: 86% comparison: 53%
	Children with serious school problems: participants: 28% comparison: 69%
Nurse home visits to high-risk mothers during pregnancy and for 2 years after birth, Elmira, New York (comparison with randomly assigned controls) University of Rochester Medical School 1978–1983	Among poor, unmarried women (N = 110): Returned or completed school, 10 months postpartum: participants: 75% controls: 50% Subsequent pregnancy, 4 years postpartum: half as many among participants as among controls Abuse or neglect of children: participants: 4% controls: 19% Among 14–16 year olds: participants (N = 28) had babies 395 gms heavier than controls (N = 17) Among mothers who smoked—premature births: participants (N = 78): 2% controls (N = 64): 10%
Summer preschool education; weekly home visits during remainder of year for black 3–5 year olds and their mothers, Murfreesboro, Tenn. (The Early Training Project) Peabody Teachers College 1962–1965	At age 21, one-third more dropouts in comparison group than among participants; control children placed in special-education classes at six times the rate of participating children
Preschool education and weekly home visits over two-year period for 3- and 4-year-old randomly assigned poor black children, Ypsilanti, Mich. (The Perry Preschool Program) High/Scope	Of 121 (N = 123) responding at age 19:

	Participants	Control
employed	59%	32%
high school graduate	67%	49%
post–high school education	38%	21%
arrested	31%	51%

1962–present; evaluation of 1962–1964 participants	Of 112 (N = 123) responding:

	years in special education	16%	28%
	Among 49 females:		
	teen-age pregnancy	32%	59%

Preschool education and enriched classes through third grade for 750 Harlem 4-year-olds; active parent support and participation Institute for Developmental Studies New York University 1963–1969	At age 21, twice as many participants as random controls were employed; one third more had high school diplomas or GED certificates; 30% more had obtained post-high school education or training

Changing elementary school climate through applying principles of child development and basic management; new relationships among principal, teachers, parents, New Haven, Conn. Yale University Child Study Center 1968–present	At outset, intervention schools ranked thirty-second and thirty-third of 33 New Haven elementary schools in reading, math, attendance, and behavior. Fifteen years later, with no change in SES of students, demonstration schools ranked third and fifth in test scores, and had no serious behavior problems. One had best attendance record in city 4 of previous 5 years.

SOURCE: L. B. Schorr, *Within Our Reach: Breaking the Cycle of Disadvantage* (New York: Anchor Press/Doubleday, 1988).

the care and education of young children are a poor fit with current needs.[3]

While economic measures (including policies to expand jobs and job training, and the assurance of decent wages) and welfare reform are central to any broad attack on intergenerational poverty and disadvantage, they will not be successful in the absence of improved services. Just as high school graduates who are competent and willing to work cannot support a family if there are no jobs to be had at a decent wage, so expanded economic opportunities cannot be seized by young people whose health has been neglected, whose education has failed to equip them with the skills they need, and whose early lives have left them without the capacity to persevere and devoid of hope.

The nation can act sensibly to improve the prospects of disadvantaged young children by providing better care and education during the preschool years without knowing more about ultimate causes of damaging outcomes. Risk-factor research undertaken over the last two decades has shown that the assaults from an unsupportive environment interact with individual vulnerabilities and multiply each others' destructive effects.[4] Rutter, for example, found that children who encountered only one risk factor were no more likely to suffer serious consequences than children experiencing no risk factors at all. When two or more stresses (constitutional or environmental) occurred together, however, the chance of a damaging outcome went up at least fourfold, and when four risk factors were present, the risk of damage increased tenfold.[5]

These findings suggest that the prevention of damage among children growing up at risk is not a matter of all or nothing; the elimination of some risk factors will help, even if others remain. Long-term outcomes could be changed if the incidence of low birthweight were reduced, if the isolated mother were helped to respond to her difficult infant, or if more children were to come to school better prepared.

We also know that such damaging outcomes as adolescent childbearing, delinquency, and dropout can be reliably predicted from poor school performance and truancy *as early as third grade.*[6] Research has further established that trouble at third grade correlates with low weight at birth, untreated health problems, failure to develop warm, secure, trusting relationships early in life, and inadequate language and coping skills at school entry.[7] For policymakers, the important news is that *every one of these risk factors has been successfully attacked through interventions we know how to provide.*

Evidence from health, social services, family support, child care, and preschool education programs shows that damaging outcomes and the risk factors that precede them can be substantially reduced by early intervention. The findings of numerous studies relating interventions to outcomes are so convergent that they cannot be explained by the possibility of methodological flaws or idiosyncratic circumstance. As shown in Table 1:

School-based health clinics have reduced the rate of teenage childbearing in St. Paul and in Baltimore.[8]

Comprehensive prenatal care reduced the number of underweight babies born in thirteen low-income counties in California, and among teenagers in Baltimore and in rural South Carolina.[9]

Family-support programs resulted in fewer children removed from home, and in lower rates of child abuse and welfare dependence in Washington State, New York State, and New Haven, Connecticut.[10]

Follow-ups into adulthood of children who had been enrolled in preschool programs found that participants—compared with control groups—included fewer children needing remedial education, fewer dropouts, fewer delinquents, fewer teenage pregnancies, and fewer youngsters unemployed in Tennessee, Michigan, and New York.[11]

The canard that in the world of social programs "nothing works" is in fact a canard, a myth that cannot be maintained in the face of the research and experience now at hand.

ATTRIBUTES OF EFFECTIVE PROGRAMS

The burgeoning evidence showing *that* there are programs that work has become more salient for policymakers because so much more is now also known about *how* and *why* they work.[12]

Successful programs are comprehensive and intensive.   They provide directly or are an easy portal to a wide array of services, delivered flexibly and coherently. Disadvantaged and depleted families typically do not have the energy or skills to negotiate their way through a daunting maze of fragmented and distant services, each with its own eligibility determinations, waiting times, and other hoops to jump through. For them, a comprehensive array of services is much more important than for middle-class families.

In the care of high-risk pregnant women, for example, the staples of middle-class prenatal care — routine lab tests and regular monitoring of blood pressure and fetal growth — are not enough. A teenager who is poor, frightened, depressed, and perhaps addicted or without a permanent home requires a great deal more than conventional obstetrical medicine if she is to have a healthy baby and get the help she needs to prepare to care for her child.[13]

Conventional parent education is another intervention that is often quite irrelevant to socially isolated and otherwise seriously disadvantaged parents. The mother who needs the most help with parenting — because she is poor, overwhelmed, and also addicted, or perhaps was profoundly neglected during her own childhood — is unlikely to find the information offered by most parenting classes very useful.[14]

Similarly, as the nation contemplates new policies to expand accessible and affordable day care, it will not be enough to meet the demand of parents and employers and welfare reformers for child care that will simply allow adults to work, important as that objective is. For most middle-class children, child care arrangements that meet minimum standards of health and safety will be good enough. For children growing up in persistent or concentrated poverty, however, the odds of school success will depend on adequate staff/child ratios and on the program's ability to provide health, nutrition, and social services, to work successfully with parents, and to focus on children's developmental needs.[15] The children who do not learn at home the preschool basics of time and space, cause and effect, now and later, trust and reciprocity, the children who have not discovered that "when I cry they will come, when I hear the water running, I will be bathed" — these are the children who do not bring to school the "social capital" required to become well educated.[16] These are the children for whom quality child care in the preschool years can make the difference between a high and a very low chance of school success.

While the importance of *comprehensiveness* and *intensiveness* may seem obvious, when funds are scarce, there are powerful pressures to dissect a successful program and select some one part to be operated in isolation, even though it was the sum of the parts that accounted for the demonstrated success.[17] The yearning for quick fixes and cheap short-cuts persists, even though isolated snippets of service, designed to solve single, narrowly circumscribed problems, are no match for the complex, deeply rooted tangles of troubles that beset overwhelmed families. Fragments of services — a few classes in parent education, a one-visit evaluation at a mental health center, or a hurried encounter with an unfamiliar and overburdened physician — are often so inadequate that they can be a waste of precious resources. When it comes to preventing profound damage among the nation's disadvantaged youth, there are no analogues to polio vaccine.

In successful programs, staff have the time, training, and skills necessary to build relationships of trust and respect with children and families.   Leaders of successful programs uniformly emphasize the importance of relationships. They know that *how* services are provided is as important as *what* is provided. They stress that working in a setting that allows them to provide services ungrudgingly is among the keys to their success.

Professionals in these programs also emphasize their collaborative posture, listening to parents, exchanging information rather than instructing, and readiness to help parents gain greater control over their own lives and to act more effectively on behalf of their children.

Successful programs deal with the child as part of a family, and the family as part of a neighborhood and community.   The nurse in a high-quality day care program not only responds to an infant's recurrent diarrhea, but sees beyond the patient before her to ask whether the child's health is threatened by circumstances that suggest the need for help to the family in the form of support or other kinds of nonmedical services. The successful school enlists parents in collaborative efforts to give children reasons to learn.

Successful programs, whether they begin with a focus on children or on their parents, generally evolve into an explicitly *two-generational* approach. They offer support to parents who need help with their lives as adults before they can make good use of services for their children. They take into account the world inhabited by those they serve — rural health clinics deliver clean water, home visitors help young mothers plan their return to school or employment while teaching them about feeding the baby, and the Head Start teacher knows when a family is threatened with eviction.

Successful programs cross long-standing professional and bureaucratic boundaries. They are prepared to offer a wide variety of services, in nontraditional settings, including homes, and at nontraditional hours. They aim to reach populations at risk rather than targeting their services on children individually identified as at risk, knowing that attempts to select the children who are at greatest risk from among a population of high-risk children can drain the energies and resources of both families and service providers, without actually improving the circumstances of the children and their families.[18] In the most effective programs, staff apply their ingenuity to getting people *into* the program, not keeping them out.

Nurses may provide family support, social workers collaborate with teachers and physicians, and psychologists listen to a mother's anxieties about her children in the course of taking her to market. No one says, "This may be what you need, but helping you get it is not part of my job or outside our jurisdiction."

PROGRAM EXAMPLES

Brief sketches of a few programs help to illustrate how these attributes are combined in successful programs.

1.　A Head Start program in Baltimore serves children who have a history of lead poisoning. The children's breakfast and lunch at the center are planned around their special nutritional needs, and their activities emphasize the structure, stimulation, and verbal exchange that are absent from many of their lives. Next door, the mothers meet with staff who help them acquire new parenting skills and new approaches to nutrition. The pediatric department that sponsors the program works with the local health and housing agencies to get the lead paint out of the homes.[19]

2.　Homebuilders, begun by a small Catholic family service agency in Tacoma, Washington, and now spreading to other parts of the country, works to keep together families threatened with the removal of a child as a result of neglect or abuse. It sees families — mainly in their own homes — during crises, usually over a period of up to six or eight weeks. Its masters' level professionals have case loads of no more than two or three families at a time. Even with that kind of intensive professional investment, Homebuilders calculates that they have been able to save, in out-of-home placements prevented, three times the cost of the Homebuilders service. In contemplating how one can justify help that is so intensive, it is useful to consider that intensive medical care — at much higher costs — for fragile newborn or aged patients barely clinging to life encounters very little public resistance. Intensive care for fragile families may one day be seen as meriting similar support.[20]

3.　The multidisciplinary, community-wide efforts of the Department of Pediatrics at the King-Drew Medical Center in the Watts area of Los Angeles include training personnel for ninety day-care centers in the surrounding community, and — in collaboration with the Los Angeles public schools — running a magnet high school in the health sciences right on the grounds of the hospital.[21]

4.　In the Appalachian community of Elmira, New York, the intervention is done by nurse home visitors, trained by the University of Rochester to help poor and isolated young mothers through their pregnancy, delivery, and early care of their babies. When the program began, rates of child abuse and neglect had reached the highest recorded level in the state as employment in heavy industry declined. The nurses made home visits, beginning during pregnancy. The focus was not only on health and nutrition; they helped the mothers prepare for their role as parents as well. They were specifically trained in the skills needed to respond to every kind of economic, physical, and emotional stress, and to help the young mothers to build bridges to other sources of professional as well as informal support. The effects of the program, as shown by comparison with similar families, randomly selected, were dramatic reductions in the proportion of babies born too soon and too small, in the incidence of child abuse, neglect, and accidents, in the rate of subsequent pregnancies and welfare dependence; and dramatic increases in the number of teenage mothers returning to school and employment.[22]

EXTENDING THE REACH OF SUCCESSFUL PROGRAMS

As one looks at the attributes of programs that succeed with seriously disadvantaged families, it is clear that they are, in some fundamental sense, anomalies in today's human service systems.

A few, like Head Start and the WIC nutrition program, already operate on a national scale, but most of the big successes are small in scale, and have in some way been shielded from the normal functioning of bureaucracies. They have, for the most part, developed in unusual conditions, and have been able to operate free from the usual outside constraints. They flourish under a variety of "protective bubbles," and have been able to take risks that would be virtually unthinkable in most large human service systems.

If the flexible, comprehensive, intensive, and personalized approaches so crucial to successful programs are to survive in mainstream human service systems, the following changes are essential: better methods of assessing program efficiency and of assuring accountability; reforms of policies and regulations to encourage, rather than undermine, efforts to provide coherent services; intensive technical assistance to help professionals and administrators cross outmoded disciplinary and bureaucratic boundaries; and new funds to expand and build on successful programs.

PROGRAM EVALUATION AND ACCOUNTABILITY

Large budget deficits, fears of wasting money and perpetuating dependency, and a gloomy sense of social problems beyond solution have combined to reinforce demands for tangible evidence of effectiveness as a condition for support of any social program.

Unfortunately, the reasonable demand for evidence that something good is happening as a result of the investment of funds often exerts unreasonable pressures to convert both program input and outcomes into whatever can be readily measured. This rush to quantify drives programs into achieving success by ducking hard cases, and into undertaking evaluation research that asks trivial questions and sacrifices significance for precision.[23] Few academics, educators, and human services administrators have caught up with the insights coming out of the management literature, which suggests that American business has often been handicapped by its practices of considering as "facts" only the data one could put numbers on, assuming that a truly rational analysis bypasses "all the messy human stuff," and striving for precision by so reducing the scope of what is analyzed that the most important questions are ignored.[24]

If *how* services are delivered is as important as *that* they are delivered, if a clinician's "skillful listening, empathy, warmth and attentive interest" are central to good and appropriate care, judging accomplishments by counting units of services provided may not be very illuminating.[25]

Program objectives like the development of warm and trusting relationships, found to be an essential attribute of virtually all programs serving high-risk families, are often sacrificed because they are so much harder to reduce to quantifiable terms than counting the number of children enrolled or scoring their performance on IQ tests. Some highly salient program outcomes, such as the effect of preschool education on increasing the chances of high school completion, or the effect of family support on reducing the incidence of delinquency, are difficult and expensive to document because of the distance in time and place between intervention and outcome. As with most investments in growth, the returns on preventive interventions in childhood come years later—and do not show up on the budget of the agency making the investment.

These knotty problems of demonstrating program effectiveness and cost savings should not have to be solved by individual service providers. They should be tackled by experts who are insulated from the daily pressures of delivering services, but fully tuned in to the real-world context in which programs operate and resources are allocated.

REFORMED POLICIES FOR PROVISION OF COHERENT SERVICES

In the provision of social and other human services, the prevailing extreme fragmentation of tasks, clientele, and funding sources means that efforts to coordinate services at the local agency level and make them available to families in some coherent way are so time-consuming, costly, and difficult that the effort is almost impossible to sustain. Federal, state, and local laws and regulations contain a myriad of obstacles to establishing and maintaining effective programs for disadvantaged populations.

These barriers must be systematically identified, and removed wherever their removal can be reconciled with the fundamental purpose of the legislation.

INTENSIVE TECHNICAL ASSISTANCE

The crucial information about what works has to be continually updated, refined, and made promptly available to the growing numbers of state and local officials who seem to be increasingly open to change. Large organizations and bureaucracies need help in creating the administrative and funding environments in which comprehensive, flexible, intensive programs — even programs operating on a small scale — can flourish. This requires skilled technical assistance. To provide such assistance with a minimum of political pressure and maximum continuity, a joint public–private organization should be established. Such an organization could assemble a cadre of talented, knowledgeable, and persevering individuals to render technical assistance, and could also help to design and perform evaluations and encourage demonstrations aimed at wider replication of successful programs. (In these latter two functions it would resemble the highly respected Manpower Demonstration Research Corporation.)

FUNDS TO EXPAND AND BUILD ON SUCCESSFUL PROGRAMS

There is every reason to expand immediately the programs that now work on a national scale, like Head Start and the WIC nutrition program, to all those who are or should be eligible. The Head Start model can also be used to provide comprehensive services to much younger children, and to extend preschool programs to provide full-day child care to all eligible children. New federal funds are also needed to provide incentives to state and local agencies to modify existing programs and policies to reflect new needs and new knowledge.

In addition, federal and state agencies should allocate funds to make grants to needy communities, especially those with heavy concentrations of persistently poor families, to enable them — with ample technical assistance — to initiate comprehensive new programs, incorporating the proven attributes of successful programs and aimed wherever possible at whole neighborhoods or defined populations.

CONCLUSION

In every part of the nation, at every level of government, in every kind of private agency, there are people determined to deliver more effective services and to find new ways of crossing ancient boundaries. They are finding increasing public support for their efforts.

Political leaders may be reluctant to commit themselves to new programs in the face of budgetary pressures and an electorate still thought to be wary of massive governmental intervention, but poll after poll shows that Americans are ready to invest in helping poor children and their families.

Now that there is clear evidence that social intervention can reduce the number of children hurt by cruel beginnings, and simultaneously promote the national welfare, the nation is in a position to utilize the many tools now available to assure that the neglected children of today become the contributing citizens of tomorrow.

Notes

1 See, for example, Committee for Economic Development, *Investing in Our Children* (New York: Committee for Economic Development, 1985); *Children in Need* (New York: Committee for Economic Development, 1987); National Governors Association, *Focus on the First Sixty Months* (Washington, D.C.: National Governors Association, 1987); and U.S. Congress, House of Representatives, Select Committee on Children, Youth, and Families, "Cost-Effective Programs for Children" (Washington, D.C.: U.S. Government Printing Office, 1985).

2 I use the term *intervention* to mean "any systematic attempt to alter the course of development from either its established or predicted path." A. M. Clarke and A. D. B. Clarke, "Thirty Years of Child Psychology: A Selective Review," *Journal of Child Psychology and Psychiatry* 27, no. 6 (1986): 742.

3 See *Business Week* Special Report, "Human Capital: The Decline of America's Work Force," September 19, 1988.

4 See S. J. Suomi, "Short and Long-Term Effects of Repetitive Mother–Infant Separations on Social Development in Rhesus Monkeys," *Developmental Psychology* 19, no. 5 (September 1983): 770–86; S. K. Escalona, "Babies at Double Hazard: Early Development of Infants at Biologic and Social Risk," *Pediatrics* 70, no. 5 (November 1982): 670–76; E. E. Werner and R. S. Smith, *Vulnerable but Invincible: A Study of Resilient Children* (New York: McGraw-Hill, 1982); and A. J. Sameroff and S. McDonough, "The Role of Motor Activity in Human Cognitive and Social Development," in *Early Intake and Activity*, ed. E. Pollitt and P. Amante (New York: Liss, 1984).

5 M. Rutter, *Changing Youth in a Changing Society: Patterns of Adolescent Development and Disorder* (Cambridge: Harvard University Press, 1980).

6 L. B. Schorr, *Within Our Reach: Breaking the Cycle of Disadvantage* (New York: Anchor Press/Doubleday, 1988), pp. 221, 341.

7 Ibid., pp. 66–67, 85–88, 140–52, 178–83.

8 Ibid., pp. 48–53.

9 Ibid., pp. 73–83.

10 Ibid., pp. 156–60, 163–75.

11 Ibid., 192–95. Eleven other preschool programs reviewed by the Cornell University-based Consortium of Longitudinal Studies show similar long-term outcomes. See Consortium for Longitudinal Studies, *As the Twig is Bent . . . Lasting Effects of Preschool Programs* (Hillsdale, N.J.: Lawrence Erlbaum Associates, 1983).

12 Schorr, *Within Our Reach*, pp. 256–83.

13 S. S. Brown, ed., *Prenatal Care: Reaching Mothers, Reaching Infants* (Washington, D.C.: National Academy Press, 1988).

14 N. A. Polansky et al., *Damaged Parents: An Anatomy of Child Neglect* (Chicago: The University of Chicago Press, 1981); and N. A. Polansky, "Isolation of the Neglectful Family," *American Journal of Orthopsychiatry* 49, no. 1 (January 1979): 149–52.

15 J. B. Richmond, "Disadvantaged Children: What Have They Compelled Us to Learn?" *Yale Journal of Biology and Medicine* 43 (December 1970): 127–44; and D. E. Pierson, D. K. Walker and T. Tivnan, "A School-Based Program from Infancy to Kindergarten for Children

and Their Parents," *The Personnel and Guidance Journal* 62, no. 8 (April 1984): 448-55.

16   P. B. Neubauer, *Process of Child Development* (New York: New American Library, 1976); "social capital" is James Coleman's phrase.

17   Schorr, *Within Our Reach*, pp. 174-75, 275-76.

18   J. Knitzer, "Mental Health Services to Children and Adolescents: A National View of Public Policies," *American Psychologist* 39, no. 8 (August 1984): 905-11; and idem, B. McGowan and M. L. Allen, *Children without Homes: An Examination of Public Responsibility of Children in Out-of-Home Care* (Washington, D.C.: Children's Defense Fund, 1978).

19   Schorr, *Within Our Reach*, pp. 101-03.

20   Ibid., pp. 157-61.

21   Ibid., pp. 106-10.

22   Ibid., pp. 169-75.

23   Ibid., p. 268.

24   T. J. Peters and R. H. Waterman, Jr., *In Search of Excellence: Lessons from America's Best-Run Companies* (New York: Warner Books, 1982), pp. 40-54.

25   M. Green, "The Pediatric Interview and History," in *Pediatric Diagnosis*, 4th ed., ed. M. Green and J. B. Richmond (Philadelphia: W. J. Saunders, 1986).

Is the Young Child Egocentric or Sociocentric?

PATRICK C. LEE

Teachers College, Columbia University

What is the mind and perception of the very young child like? How can the early childhood specialist best understand the sense-making potential of the child? Lee explores two antithetical views, the Piagetian egocentric view of the child developing through only its own perspective and a sociocentric view of the child's innate sociality enabling it to take and share the perspectives of others.

A puzzling disjuncture exists between theory and evidence in our current understanding of the young child's perspective-taking ability. On the one hand, there is Piaget's theory, arguably the dominant account of developmental epistemology, which maintains that the young human being is incapable of knowing anything except from its own perspective, incapable even of knowing that there is such a thing as perspective. This is the so-called egocentric view of childhood, which holds that the young child is unable to "decenter" from the perspective of its own "ego" onto that of another person. Under such circumstances, of course, it would be impossible to be social in any recognizably human way. Human sociality requires that subjects assent to the validity of other subjectivities. If the young child cannot do this, and in Piaget's theory it cannot, then it cannot be social. This is a radically individual account of how children construct knowledge of the world.

On the other side of the disjuncture, there is a growing body of empirical evidence indicating that the very young child is *not* egocentric, at least not in any structural and/or systematic sense. These findings show that young children spontaneously recognize that other perspectives exist, that other perspectives are of great interest to them, and that they will work hard to coordinate their own perspectives with those of others. The empirical evidence, in other words, portrays a child who is radically "sociocentric" and it makes a strong case for the deeply social nature of the child. Moreover, the evidence makes a persuasive case for the child's *social* construction of perspectival knowledge, and on these grounds it is quite damaging to the structural claims of Piaget's theory. That is, the more social components there are built into a task, the more precocious the child is in constructing an appreciation of the perspective of the other.

In other words, if, as Piaget's theory claims, the young child is *structurally* egocentric, then it should not matter whether perspective-taking tasks are social or asocial; the egocentric child would fail both types of task. However, if empirical research shows that the child does better in socially defined perspective-taking tasks than in those that are not social, one could not conclude that egocentricity is structural or systematic. Rather, one would have to conclude that childhood egocentricity is a creature of a certain class of tasks, those that are stripped of social content; and that young children are sociocentric in tasks that incorporate social content.

Even the most casual reading of the available research all but forces the latter conclusion. Accordingly, I will attempt to make the strong case for early childhood sociocentricity by reviewing two bodies of research, one on the child's visual perspective-taking, and the other on children's conversations. Prior to this, however, we should take a brief look at what Piaget means by egocentricity and the procedure he uses to demonstrate it in young children.

PIAGET'S ACCOUNT OF EGOCENTRICITY

It should be made clear that Piaget never intended to use the term *egocentricity* in its popular sense as a synonym for selfishness, self-centeredness, wanting to be the center of attention, or any such undesirable social or moral quality. Rather, the theory uses the term in a technical sense as referring to the young child's incapacity for decentering from its own ego in the process of constructing knowledge of the world. In the earliest months of life, the Piagetian infant is so radically egocentric that it cannot distinguish between itself (the ego) and the world. It behaves as though it understood the world to be an extension of its own perceptions, actions, and wishes. This is the period of infantile "ontological" egocentricity and, for our present purposes, it is not particularly germane.

At about eighteen or twenty months of age, according to Piaget, the infant enters the "preoperational period" and egocentricity assumes a different form.[1] By this age the toddler is able to distinguish between itself and the world, but fails to appreciate that there are many possible views of the world. That is, it fails to recognize that there are perspectives other than its own or that there is even such a thing as perspective. The preschool-age child operates as if its view of the world were *the* view of the world, the objective and only way in which the world is known. In Piaget's terms, as mentioned above, the young child is structurally incapable of decentering from its own ego's perspective and recentering on the perspective of the other person. Thus, the child behaves as if what it knows and perceives were by definition known and perceived by the other. This latter form of epistemological or perspectival egocentricity is the topic of the present article.

Piaget's classic demonstration of perspectival egocentricity is his so-called three-mountains task. In this task, the child sits at one side of a table that holds a papier-mâché construction of three mountains. Since the mountains differ in size, color, and other incidental features, the array looks quite different from each side of the table. A little doll is then placed on the side of the table to the child's right, for example, and the child is asked what the mountains look like to the doll. The child responds by pointing out one picture from a set of pictures (or, in another version, by assembling a smaller group of model mountains). Piaget and Inhelder found that children below four years of age were not able to respond to the problem at all and that five- to seven-year old children almost always selected the picture of the mountains that corresponded to their own viewpoint.[2] This was taken by Piaget to mean that the subject could not decenter from its own ego, that is, from its own viewpoint, to appreciate the perspective of the doll. In other words, the child's knowledge of the world was limited to its own viewpoint and, as far as the child could indicate, so was everyone else's knowledge.

At about seven or eight years of age, the child overcomes perspectival egocentricity and enters Piaget's "concrete operational" period. At this point the child is, according to the theory, no longer restricted to its own viewpoint, but can easily and naturally appreciate the perspectives of others. In the remaining sections of this article, I would like to present evidence that this ability in fact appears much earlier in the child's life, even as early as one or two years of age.

VISUAL PERSPECTIVE-TAKING

My position is that the major reason children have difficulty with Piaget's three-mountains task is that it is not social in nature. First, there are no other people involved in the task itself and even the doll is only minimally suggestive of imaginary personhood (it is wooden and about one inch tall). Second, the task incorporates no apparent motivation, intention, interaction, and so forth—there seems to be no scenario, human purpose, or narrative to organize the child's sense of the exercise. Finally, the child's responses are not verbally represented, but take the form of pictorial or visual representation (i.e., pictures and scale models); verbal representation is a major currency of social exchange, while pictures are not—people talk to each other, they do not communicate by pointing to pictures. If my contention that the young child has precocious social capabilities is correct, then the three-mountains task is stripped of precisely those elements—people, speech, and meaningful social content—that would enable the child to display its perspective-taking competence. Conversely, research tasks that incorporate one or more of these social elements ought to reveal a distinctly different profile of the young child's competence at taking the perspective of the other. Let us look at a number of studies of how quite young children perform in gazing, pointing, showing, and hiding tasks.[3]

GAZING AND POINTING

If, while playing with a young child, one were to gaze at an object to the side and if the child were to follow one's gaze, this would indicate that it was capable of responding to the perspective of another. The same would be true if the child looked at something one pointed to. Lempers did research on these two behaviors and found that all his twelve- and fourteen-month-old subjects looked at a nearby object an adult pointed to, and 71 percent of them looked at a distant object when an adult pointed to it. Further, he found that 88 percent of these babies could orient toward and visually locate an object that was merely gazed at by an adult.[4] Butterworth and Cochran had similar results with eighteen-month-old babies and their mothers.[5] When the mother gazed at an object to the left or right, the infant would watch the mother, track the line of her gaze, and fix its own gaze on the target object. These two studies indicate that by a year and a half of age, children have a working awareness of the perspectival initiative and independence of other people. They do not behave as if their own point of view were the one and only point of view, nor do they behave as if there were no such thing as a point of view.

Pointing, of course, works both ways. If, as seems to be the case, the infant can look at what others point out, can it also point out things to others? Leung and Rheingold studied the infant's pointing and found that at twelve and one-half months of age, half of infants pointed out objects to their mothers, and that by sixteen and one-half months they all pointed out objects.[6] Moreover, 38 percent visually checked their mothers' responses, despite the fact that they were seated so close that monitoring their mothers did not seem to be necessary. Lempers observed that 92 percent of fourteen-month-old infants pointed out objects to an adult and 64 percent visually checked to see whether the adult responded to their pointings.[7] Again, these behaviors indicate that the very young child does not egocentrically assume that another sees the world from its perspective. By pointing, the baby works to communicate its perspective and, by visually checking, it follows through to see if its communication has been understood.

One question that could be raised here is whether infants point to things as a way of guiding or amplifying their *own* looking. If so, then pointing would not indicate recognition of another's perspective. However, two findings suggest this is not the case. First, as mentioned above, a significant number of infants visually monitor the other's response to their pointing, suggesting the pointing is intended to influence what the *other* looks at. Second, Leung and Rheingold's study noted that once babies start to point, they do not attend to objects any more frequently than babies who are not yet pointing. Thus, pointing does not seem to be a device to increase the infant's own looking. Rather, it seems to be a social gesture, designed to guide and direct the other's viewing behavior. In other words, the baby's pointing is an attempt to actively draw the other into the baby's viewpoint or perspective, thus indicating that the infant makes no egocentric assumptions about the other's perspective.

In another study, Rheingold and her colleagues found that 93 percent of eighteen-month-old babies showed toys and other things to their mothers by pointing them out or holding them up.[8] These babies showed objects to their mothers an average of once every two minutes, and the more objects available (toys, mobiles, colorful posters), the more they pointed them out. Rheingold also noted that the babies often vocalized or visually checked their mothers before or after pointing. Obviously, these toddlers were strongly invested in sharing their viewpoint and their experience with their mothers and did so spontaneously and frequently. Moreover, the fact that they did not simply assume that the mother perceives what they perceive indicates that they were not egocentric.

It would seem that the infant's social pointing is an attempt to establish *intersubjectivity* with another person. A precondition to such efforts is a recognition that the other's subjectivity is distinct from the child's own subjectivity. The baby's "recognition" of the independence of subjectivities is almost surely not at the level of deliberate and rational awareness, but this does not make it any less real. The very young child evidently has a rudimentary understanding of the need to actively work to coordinate another's subjective viewpoint with its own, and vice versa. Again, the capability is completely inconsistent with an egocentric account of early childhood.

SHOWING AND HIDING

Lempers, Flavell, and Flavell did a series of investigations of how effectively young children could show things to an adult observer when they were asked to do so.[9] They found that two-year-olds were able to orient a toy so that it faced toward the observer and away from the child; three-year-olds could show a picture so that it faced the observer right side up, and had its back to the child. These findings clearly indicate that the very young child not only has an understanding of the other's perspective, but recognizes that to get it the right way for the other perspective, one has to get it the wrong way from one's own perspective. Lempers and his associates also found that two-and-one-half year olds would remove a screen so an observer could see an object, indicating that they understand that a screen can block another's view even when it does not block their own. Another interesting finding was that these children, even the three-year-olds, had a very hard time showing something to an *unseen* observer on the other side of a large screen. It may be that blocking out the other person had the effect of partially "desocializing" the task, thus hampering the child's understanding of the other's perspective. The children had to peek around the screen at the other person in order to get the task right. Of course, peeking had the affect of restoring the other person, that is, "resocializing" the task.

Hiding is the converse of showing and, just as showing requires an ability to appreciate what *can* be seen by another, hiding requires an awareness of what *cannot* be seen from another perspective. Flavell, Shipstead, and Croft found that two-and-one-half year olds were able to hide an object behind a screen so that an observer could not see it, even while they themselves could.[10] An egocentric child would simply have blocked the object from its own view on the assumption that if ego (i.e., the child) could not see it, it could not be seen at all. Lempers et al. added another interesting wrinkle to the hiding task by using large objects that the children could not move.[11] They found that three-and-one-half year olds would turn the observer around so that her back was to the large object, thus effectively "hiding" it from her.

In another study, Hughes and Donaldson devised a more complicated task than those already described.[12] They set up a cross-shaped configuration of two walls on a table, such that four compartments were formed. They then introduced two policemen dolls and one little boy doll. The two policemen were placed at various vantage points and the child was asked to "hide the boy so that both the policemen can't see him." Three-and-a-half year old children placed the doll in the correct compartment 88 percent of the time, showing that they could coordinate two perspectives, neither of which was their own. When the problem was made more difficult, involving a third wall to make five compartments, three-year-olds succeeded in hiding the boy from the policemen 60 percent of the time, and four-year-olds had a 90 percent success rate. In an even more complex version, a sixth compartment and a third policeman were added, and 70 percent of another sample of three-year-olds got it right, as did 80 percent of four-year-olds. Hughes and Donaldson also noted that very few of the children's errors were egocentric: They did not place the doll so it was hidden from themselves (an egocentric error); on the contrary, the two children who performed most poorly placed the doll in the compartment closest to them where both they and the policeman could see it very easily (a nonegocentric error).

These three- and four-year-olds were apparently quite skilled in coordinating two or three different perspectives, none of which were their own, hardly a sign of egocentricity. How were they able to do so well in so complex a task? Their remarkable success was probably due to the fact that the task was presented to them as a social one. The situation had a narrative line in which the child had to coordinate the policemen's intention to catch the boy with the boy's desire to escape detection. This scenario is easily understood by young children, as they have all at one time or another been naughty and tried to escape the consequences by hiding or some other evasive action. As Hughes and Donaldson concluded, it made basic "human sense" to the child. Characterized by motives, intentions, interactions, and narrative, the three-policemen task had precisely the kind of socially meaningful content that Piaget's three-mountains task lacked.

One final study that ought to be mentioned in this connection was done by Ives.[13] He gave children two ways of responding to a perspective-taking situation that, while less complex than the three-mountains task, was similar to it in format. Ives placed an object (e.g., a toy boat, a toy horse) on a table with the child seated at one side and a camera placed at various angles to the object. Some of the children were asked to describe in words which side of the toy the camera would photograph and others were asked to choose from a group of pictures which one the camera would take. The results were remarkable: 89.5 percent of three-year-olds got it right when they could respond in words, while only 38 percent got it right when they had to select a picture — all the more surprising since it was presented as a "picture-taking" task. For five-year-olds the correct response rates were 92.5 and 51 percent, respectively, indicating that both age groups were much more precocious in the verbal mode than in a pictorial mode similar to the one used by Piaget in the three-mountains task. From a sociocentric perspective, these results make good sense: Words are an important currency of social interaction. Children communicate with others in words, not by pointing to pictures. Thus, as Ives's task demonstrates, the more social the representational mode used, the more precocious is the child's performance.

What the foregoing studies seem to indicate is that visual perspective-taking tasks are arranged along a continuum from the socially rich to the socially impoverished. The more social components built into the task format — actual people, familiar people (e.g., the child's mother), the verbal representational mode, presenting the task as a social problem (e.g., the policemen-and-boy scenario) — the more precocious is the child's perspective-taking ability. Conversely, to the extent that the perspective-taking format is stripped of social components, as in Piaget's three-mountains task, the older the child has to be to perform adequately. The more social character the task has, the less egocentric the child is.

CONVERSATIONAL PERSPECTIVE-TAKING

If there is an inverse relation between the social character of a situation and the child's manifestation of egocentricity, then it would be particularly revealing to see how young children perform in what may be the most social of tasks: the conversation. A sociocentric account would predict that the young child would have a precocious appreciation of the perspective of a conversational partner, while an egocentric account would predict the opposite. The available research evidence clearly favors the sociocentric view.

Researchers on conversational perspective-taking have addressed three basic questions: (1) Does the child speak differently to adults, age mates, and younger children? (2) If so, do its speech adjustments indicate a sensitivity to the needs or characteristics of the listener? (3) Does it adjust its speech to what is actually said and meant by the other? For example, regarding the first two questions, if five-year-olds were to speak more simply to two-year-olds than to adults, this would suggest that they make appropriate distinctions between the linguistic and cognitive capacities of these two kinds of listeners. It would indicate, to use Piaget's term, that the young child can decenter onto the perspective of the other and modify its verbal communication accordingly.

In a ground-breaking study of children's conversations, Shatz and Gelman found that four-year-old children speak similarly to adults and peers, but that they speak to two-year-olds in shorter and grammatically simpler phrases and use more attention-fixing statements—particularly the expressions "see," "look," and "watch"—in their talk with two-year-olds.[14] Moreover, the younger the child addressed is (i.e., less than twenty-eight months of age), the greater are the "downward" adjustments in speech made by the four-year-old. In a similar study, Sachs and Devin noted that young children (age three-and-one-half to five-and-one-half years) speak to toddlers in shorter and less complex utterances than those used in speaking to adults and peers.[15] Children also address toddlers more often by name to get and hold their attention, and they use more imperatives and baby talk with toddlers. One particularly revealing finding was that, although children ask rather few questions of toddlers, the ones they do ask are mostly directed to the youngster's internal wants, needs, and likes (e.g., "Do you want some?"). In contrast, most questions asked of adults and peers are addressed to information or events in the external world (e.g., "Where is the fireman?"). It is clear that these young children have a theory about toddlers: that they are creatures of their wants and needs and know little about the world, and that questions taking their perspective into account must be shaped by these factors. Not a particularly flattering theory, perhaps, but not an egocentric one either.

In another study, Dunn and Kendrick recorded the speech of three-year-olds to their mothers and to their one-year-old siblings.[16] They found that the children spoke in shorter phrases to their siblings and used two to four times as much repetition and attention-getting discourse with their siblings as with their mothers. The children also used many more verbal prohibitions, directives, and restraints with their siblings than with their mothers, showing an appropriate understanding of directions of social authority and responsibility. In fact, Dunn and Kendrick noted that the three-year-olds had a good sense for the conversational incapacity of their fourteen-month-old siblings: Spoken, turn-taking conversation was infrequent, even though, on a *nonverbal* level, reciprocal interactions were fairly common. These thirty-four- to thirty-six-month-old youngsters recognized that their siblings' immaturity required (or at least permitted) a "talking down" that was markedly different from the "talking up" strategies they used with their mothers.

Taken together, these three studies paint a fairly consistent picture of the adjustments three- to five-year-old children make in their verbal interactions with others of different ages. When the listener is younger, the child uses simpler syntax, shorter phrases, fewer questions, and more imperatives, repetition, and attention-getting utterances. The exact opposite pattern holds for older listeners.

How is it that children so young can make such a sophisticated set of adjustments? It may be that they simply imitate the way adults talk to babies and toddlers; or they may adjust their speech to fit fixed stereotypes they have about listeners, using the "adult mode" of talk with adults, automatically switching into the "baby mode" with babies, and so forth. Or, as I have been arguing here, young children may be genuinely able to take the perspective of the other; that is, they can adjust to the actual construction of meaning as it occurs in a particular conversation with a particular other. Of course, these three explanations are not mutually exclusive. There is no reason in principle that the perspective-taking child would not acquire interactional strategies through imitating adults. Nor is there any reason that he or she would not use stereotypes as rules of thumb for starting and organizing conversations with others of different ages. After all, not every conversationalist is assessed *de novo*. Even adult conversation is characterized by formulaic constructions and preformed attitudes about categories of listeners. Still, to the extent that one could invoke imitation or listener-stereotypy as explanations of the child's pattern of speech adjustments, one would tend to diminish the case for the child's conversational perspective-taking. Let us look briefly at imitation and somewhat more extensively at stereotypy as alternative accounts.

IMITATION VERSUS PERSPECTIVE-TAKING

In their study, Dunn and Kendrick looked very closely at how mothers speak to younger siblings in order to compare mother-to-baby talk with child-to-baby talk.[17] They found that, as a proportion of total speech, children used about twice as many repetitions and attention-getting phrases with their younger siblings as their mothers did, and mothers asked ten times as many questions as children did. Of 877 child-to-baby verbalizations only 32 (i.e.,

3.6 percent) were full or partial imitations of the mothers'. This low level of imitation is remarkable since, as Dunn and Kendrick point out, most children are extremely interested in their mothers' interactions with their younger siblings and often watch what goes on very attentively. In this connection, it is also noteworthy that Shatz and Gelman found that children *without* siblings spoke to toddlers the same way as children who did have siblings.[18] Obviously, the former had less opportunity to imitate their mothers' way of talking to a younger child since there was no younger child at home.

Although these findings indicate that young children do not directly imitate their mothers phrase for phrase, they do not rule out the possibility that children indirectly imitate the "maternal role" or the general posture mothers take toward younger siblings. Even if they do engage in role imitation, however, and it is completely plausible that they would, they seem to do a selective job of it. For example, children overemphasize repetitions and attention-seizing strategies, while underemphasizing questions. This is clearly a selective pattern of imitation and it may be in the service of the three-year-old's psychological need to demonstrate the relative degrees of competence between itself and its fourteen-month-old sibling. If such communicative displays do satisfy such needs, however, they are also an accurate reading of the characteristics of the one-year-old listener. One-year-olds are in fact less competent than three-year-olds. The three-year-old does not ask questions of the one-year-old because, unlike the mother, it is not in the business of enhancing the embryonic conversation skills of the baby. The mother seems to overestimate the baby's conversational competence — in fact, she herself answers many of the questions for the baby — because she sees it as a way of relating to the baby or teaching it, or both.

In any event, these findings do not encourage the conclusion that imitation is the major determinant of the adjustments children make when talking with younger children. On the contrary, they indicate that the child has a self-regulated ability to appreciate the baby's characteristics, rather than a parrotlike talent for saying to babies what adults say to babies.

STEREOTYPY VERSUS PERSPECTIVE TAKING

Even if children do not directly imitate adults, might it be that they merely stereotype different categories of listeners? That is, might the child adjust not to the particular conversationalist, but to a stereotyped version of the conversationalist? If so, it could be argued that children talk differently to babies and adults not because of anything that is actually *said*, or even because of who they are, but because of *what* they are.

Several years ago, Masur conducted a study that sheds some light on this question.[19] She analyzed the verbal interactions between four- and two-year-olds and discovered an interesting two-step process. In the first part of an interaction the four-year-old tends to adjust the length of its statements to how verbally productive the two-year-old is, such that two-year-olds who themselves produce longer phrases are spoken to in longer phrases. Then, as the interaction proceeds, the four-year-olds shift from how talkative their two-year-old partners are to how *responsive* they are to the conversational topic. Those two-year-olds who are more responsive are spoken to in syntactically more complex ways, while those who are less responsive receive less complex verbal input from the four-year-olds. Thus, four-year-olds apparently do not treat all two-year-olds as an undifferentiated category. Their speech adjustments seem to be based at first on a gross assessment of the younger child's verbal productivity, and then on a more refined assessment of his or her ability to participate responsively in a topic-organized interaction. This suggests a remarkable attentiveness to the language and dialogical capabilities of the *specific* other and an ability to adapt accordingly.

Cox suggests an even more refined approach to this issue, that is, that we look at adjustments made in the flow of a particular conversation.[20] Unfortunately, there is little if any published evidence of this sort for child-to-younger-child conversation, but there are some data on peer dialogue and child-to-adult conversations. However, it should be mentioned that, on this point, it matters little what the age of the listener is. If the young child adjusts to actual communication problems that crop up in a particular exchange, then the adjustments must be in response to the particular flow or disruption of meaning rather than to a fixed stereotype of the conversationalist.

Keenan and Kline did extensive observations of the spontaneous conversation of a pair of thirty-three-month-old twins.[21] They noted that these boys, typical for children in their age range, were very concerned to establish joint attention to the same topic. At this age, one child does not like to go on in conversation without a clear signal from the other that they are on the same topic. For example, the one may assert "Big one, no, big one" and the other is likely to respond "Big one." Keenan and Kline found that this actual conversational formula of assertion-repetition is very frequently followed. In the two children they studied, assertions were followed by repetitions 57 percent of the time. What is interesting for our purposes is how hard these young children will work to establish a common topic. Here is an example from Keenan and Kline:

CHILD A:	goosey goosey gander . . .
CHILD B:	moth moth
CHILD A:	goosey goosey gander, where shall I wander . . .
CHILD B:	moth moth moth moth
CHILD A:	upstairs downstairs in the lady's chamber . . .
CHILD B:	moth moth moth
CHILD A:	moth?
CHILD B:	gone moth allgone[22]

It seems obvious that Child B keeps repeating the word "moth" because he assesses, quite correctly, his peer's topic as different from his own. And it is only when Child A repeats the key word that Child B is satisfied that their perspectives are sufficiently shared that he can proceed with his communication that the moth has flown away:

CHILD B: gone moth allgone
CHILD A: two moths
CHILD B: many moths
CHILD A: mmm many moths, mmm many moths
CHILD B: he goed on the ceiling
CHILD A: gone[23]

Again, this extraordinary attention to establishing a shared topic, and doing so successfully, indicates that these thirty-three-month-old boys are not egocentric. If they were, each would simply assume the centrality of his viewpoint and engage in what Piaget calls a "collective monologue."[24]

Another recurring phenomenon in young children's conversations with each other and with adults is the request for clarification. Cox reports a conversation between herself and her twenty-six-month-old daughter, who was eating a tea cake. They are sitting at a café table:

CHILD: I'm puttin lots in
MOTHER: What did you say?   (turning towards her)
CHILD: I'm putting lots in
MOTHER: I don't understand   (shaking head, puzzled expression)
          What did you say?
CHILD: I got too *much*
MOTHER: Oh yes, you must be careful not to put too much in. You
          might choke.[25]

The first time the mother requests clarification the child interprets the request as not having heard what she said. So she repeats it. Then the mother rephrases her request ("I don't understand. *What* did you say?") and the child reinterprets it, this time correctly, as meaning her mother did not understand what she was talking about. So she rephrases the topic, shifting emphasis from how much tea cake she was eating to how much she had on the table. The mother then "gets it" and responds to the child's initial concern about how much she was "puttin in." This is a revealing example of how a very young child is both inclined and able to assess the perspective of the other in the service of establishing conversational coherence.

In another study, Garvey and Hogan looked at, among other things, the use of the "summons–answer routine" as a conversational opener between children three-and-one-half to five-and-one-half years of age.[26] This routine usually takes a three-step form: an attention solicitation by the first speaker (the summons), an attentive response by the second speaker (the answer), an introduction of a topic by the first speaker. One simple example noted by Garvey and Hogan is:

CHILD A: You know what?
CHILD B: What?
CHILD A: Sometime you can come to my house.[27]

Garvey and Hogan found that 77 percent of these routines were well formed, that is, pursued, as above, to completion. This suggests that, even in the preschool years, children are in the process of using and mastering certain dialogical formulas for the purpose of transforming their separate perspectives into shared topics. The summons–answer sequence is a highly routinized formula, needless to say, and we have all heard children use it over and over. This is precisely the point: The everydayness of the formula shows that for young children perspectival divergence is so taken for granted that it is dealt with in a routine and repetitive fashion. In fact, it is so routine that departures from the formula can lead to great surprises, as in this example:

CHILD A: Do you know what?
CHILD B: What? (pause, B turns to A and moves toward him)
          What? (repetition is louder, with broader rising–falling intonation)
CHILD A: (grins and laughs before speaking)
          You're a nut.
CHILD B: What? What? What's a nut? What?
          (A and B laugh simultaneously, B dashes threateningly at A, shrieking the final "what?")[28]

This dialogue has three remarkable features. First, although child A's ostensible point is to introduce a topic ("Do you know what?"), it is the listener, child B, who works to get the topic introduced (repeating the word "what?"), even though it is not her topic. She is obviously trying to get at what is on Child A's mind, and, by repeating herself, is adjusting to the pause in A's communication. Second, Child A creatively breaks the formula in order to play a verbal joke on B. He waits for B to repeat herself so as to draw her more deeply into the as yet unknown topic. Her additional commitment to the topic intensifies the effect of the joke. Finally, Child B, in her last statement ("What? What? What's a nut?") seems to be trying to expunge the joke by going back to the second step of the formula, even as she realizes, much to her shock and delight, that the formula has been skillfully broken, the topic has been established ("What's a nut?"), and the joke is on her.

In these several examples taken from actual dialogues, it is clear that the young child is capable of adjusting its speech in terms of the particular, unfolding construction of meaning in a given conversation, and that these adjustments are not in response to a preformed stereotype of the other. If anything, a good number of the child's adjustments seem to be in response to (and organized by) emergent conversational formulas that are designed specifically to coordinate separate perspectives; although, as the above example shows, even fairly standardized routines can be intentionally and meaningfully broken for the purpose of surprise and humor.

It is also clear that child conversationalists, perhaps more so than adults, work very hard at getting and giving signals that indicate the degree to which they are both on the same topic. The young children excerpted above are capable of co-constructing effective (albeit distinctly childlike) dialogue because they are engaged in a more or less continuous assessment of the other's perspective as it is revealed in the other's words. In fact, the ability to take the perspective of the other is a necessary precondition to the kind of dialogue that is routinely and spontaneously achieved by young children.

CONCLUSION

In fairness to Piaget's theory, two points ought to be made. First, in its mature version, the theory is primarily an account of the development of physical knowledge, not of social knowledge. That is, it describes the emergence of the logical and conceptual structures of thought that organize the child's sensory-motor and mental *actions on* the world of *physical objects*. This is physical knowledge. It does not account, except in a secondary and derivative sense, for the mental structures that organize and guide the child's *interactions with* the world of *human subjects*. This latter is social knowledge. Second, it views the child as an individual actor who, in essential isolation, reinvents the logical basis of scientific thinking. It does not view the child as a culturally, historically, and socially embedded interactor who co-constructs its mental life in negotiation with other similarly embedded persons. Although Piaget seems to take the position that there is continuity between the structures of physical and social knowledge,[29] the overwhelming emphasis of his theoretical and empirical work is on the former set of structures, particularly as the theory reached its most mature and systematic version in his later years of work. Thus, we should not expect Piaget's theory to "naturally" assign priority to the explanation of social events, nor generate social constructs to explain physical knowledge. It is not explicitly a theory of social modes of knowing, even though, in the interest of completeness, it may occasionally pretend to be. The child's social life has no central theoretical significance for Piaget.

Although Piaget remained committed to the notion of egocentricity in some of his latter writings, by his own admission it has run into problems of understanding and acceptance.[30] I would like to suggest that, for practical purposes, Piaget's position on perspectival egocentricity can be dismissed, even while we may be well instructed by his account of the development of physical knowledge.[31] I would maintain, however, that to the extent Piaget's theory posits the child as an individual inventor of knowledge, it is only a partial account even of the formation of physical knowledge. What is needed is a more adequate theory, one that specifically accounts for the empirical findings on the child's sociocentricity and generally embraces the deeply social nature of the child's construction of knowledge. This leads to a concluding point.

The evidence clearly indicates that the child is a more precocious perspective taker in social than in nonsocial situations, but I have not yet addressed the question of why this is so. The answer to this question lies in recognizing that, as an idea, perspective *logically* implies the existence of another way of viewing things. This, in turn, *socio-logically* implies the existence and participation of other people, given the reality and ubiquity of human sociality. In fact, other people are, for all practical purposes, inescapable in the child's life, particularly when it comes to experiences that involve perspective, communication, reciprocity, and so forth. Thus, like any social activity, perspective is not an individual construction. Rather, it is a joint construction or a co-construction and, as such, is facilitated by the actual presence of another. This is explicitly the case in conversation and pointing, where the participants actively help in the co-construction of each other's perspective; and it is implicitly so in tasks such as hiding and showing, where a present other serves to confirm or disconfirm the child's hypotheses about perspective. So many social elements are built into the tasks discussed earlier—a participating other person, the use of communicative speech, narratives of socially interacting characters—that the child's perspective-taking becomes effectively co-constructive even when the participating researcher attempts to take a posture of "scientific neutrality." Once the researcher enters the perspective-taking task itself, its outcome is necessarily co-constructed.

Vygotsky offers a deeper theoretical appreciation of the social construction of perspective, in his account of the "Zone of Proximal Development" (ZPD).[32] Among other things, the ZPD incorporates the commonsensical insight that whatever a child does with the help of a more competent other (i.e., actual help, not "interfering" help) is superior to what it can do on its own. If this proposition holds, as Vygotsky intended, for mental performances that are not social per se (e.g., the construction of a puzzle),[33] then it would hold even more strongly for specifically social performances. When the form of knowledge used by the child—in this case, perspective-taking—is itself inherently social, then its proper and most appropriate context would be one that involves social interaction. A more adequate theoretical account, such as Vygotsky's, would help us to understand why, as empirical research demonstrates, socially construed perspective-taking tasks do not show the young child to be egocentric. On the contrary they reveal very young children to be remarkably and precociously sociocentric.

Notes

1   For a succinct overview of Piaget's developmental theory, see Jean Piaget and Bärbel Inhelder, *The Psychology of the Child* (New York: Basic Books, 1969).

2   Jean Piaget and Bärbel Inhelder, *The Child's Conception of Space* (London: Routledge & Kegan Paul, 1956), chap. 8.

3   For a review of the research on perspective-taking, see M. V. Cox, *The Child's Point of View: The Development of Cognition and Language* (New York: St. Martin's Press, 1986), pp. 3–90.

4   Jacques D. Lempers, "Young Children's Productions and Comprehension of Nonverbal Deictic Behaviors," *The Journal of Genetic Psychology* 135 (1979): 93–102.

5   George E. Butterworth and E. Cochran, "Towards a Mechanism of Joint Visual Attention in Human Infancy," *International Journal of Behavorial Development* 3 (1980): 253–72.

6   Eleanor H. L. Leung and Harriet L. Rheingold, "Development of Pointing as a Social Gesture," *Developmental Psychology* 17, no. 2 (1981): 215–20.

7   Lempers, "Young Children's Productions," pp. 97–98.

8   Harriet L. Rheingold, Dale F. Hay, and Meredith J. West, "Sharing in the Second Year of Life," *Child Development* 47 (1976): 1148–58.

9   Jacques D. Lempers, E. R. Flavell, and J. H. Flavell, "The Development in Very Young Children of Tacit Knowledge concerning Visual Perception," *Genetic Psychology Monographs* 95 (1977): 3–53.

10   John H. Flavell, Susan G. Shipstead, and Karen Croft, "Young Children's Knowledge about Visual Perception: Hiding Objects from Others," *Child Development* 49 (1978): 1208–11.

11   Lempers et al., "The Development . . . of Tacit Knowledge," pp. 3–53.

12   Martin Hughes and Margaret Donaldson, "The Use of Hiding Games for Studying the Coordination of Viewpoints," *Educational Review* 31, no. 2 (1979): 133–40.

13   William Ives, "Preschool Children's Ability to Coordinate Spatial Perspectives through Language and Pictures," *Child Development* 51, no. 4 (December 1980): 1303–06.

14   Marilyn Shatz and Rochel Gelman, "The Development of Communication Skills: Modifications in the Speech of Young Children as a Function of Listener," *Monographs of the Society for Research in Child Development* 38, no. 5 (October 1973): 1–38.

15   Jacqueline Sachs and Judith Devin, "Young Children's Use of Age-appropriate Speech Styles in Social Interaction and Role-playing," *Journal of Child Language* 3 (1976): 81–98.

16   Judy Dunn and Carol Kendrick, "The Speech of Two- and Three-year-olds to Infant Siblings: 'Baby Talk' and the Context of Communication," *Journal of Child Language* 9 (1982): 579–95.

17   Ibid.

18   Shatz and Gelman, "The Development of Communication Skills," p. 11.

19   Elise Frank Masur, "Preschool Boys' Speech Modifications: The Effect of Listeners' Linguistic Levels and Conversational Responsiveness," *Child Development* 49 (1978): 924–27.

20   Cox, *The Child's Point of View*, p. 57.

21   Elinor Ochs Keenan and Ewan Klein, "Coherency in Children's Discourse," *Journal of Psycholinguistic Research* 4, no. 4 (1975): 365–80.

22   Ibid., p. 371.

23   Ibid., p. 375.

24   Piaget and Inhelder, *The Psychology of the Child*, pp. 120–21.

25   Cox, *The Child's Point of View*, p. 66.

26   Catherine Garvey and Robert Hogan, "Social Speech and Social Interaction: Egocentrism Revisited," *Child Development* 44 (1973): 562–68.

27   Ibid., p. 566.

28   Ibid.

29   See, for example, Piaget and Inhelder, *The Psychology of the Child*, where the authors claim that "the decentering which is a prerequisite for the formation of the operations applies

not only to a physical universe . . . but also *necessarily* to an interpersonal or social universe" (p. 95, italics added). Interestingly enough, however, in a specific discussion of egocentrism later in the same book, Piaget and Inhelder use more qualified language, referring to a "*possible* analogy" between interpersonal and intrapersonal actions and stating that egocentrism in social exchanges is "highly *probable*" (p. 118, italics added).

30   Ibid., pp. 61 and 118.

31   Note that I separate the main body of the theory from its position on egocentricity on practical grounds only. On logical grounds internal to the theory, this separation would be more difficult and, perhaps, impossible. It would require a careful consideration of the role of emphasis versus system in theory building, the relation of Piaget's epistemology to his psychology, and the implications of "centering" and "decentering" as pervasive properties of the preoperational period. See also note 29 above.

32   L. S. Vygotsky, *Mind in Society: The Development of Higher Psychological Processes* (Cambridge: Harvard University Press, 1978), pp. 84–91.

33   James V. Wertsch, "From Social Interaction to Higher Psychological Processes: A Clarification and Application of Vygotsky's Theory," *Human Development* 22 (1979): 1–22.

Kindergarten: Current Circumstances Affecting Curriculum

DORIS PRONIN FROMBERG

Hofstra University

What should we teach young children? Should we strive to develop general intellectual skills or introduce them to formal academic subjects? Should the classroom be a formal-traditional environment or an open-experiential one? How do current certification and administrative practices affect the kindergarten education of young children? Fromberg answers these questions in her essay on the kindergarten curriculum.

It makes sense to consider kindergarten in any discussion of early childhood education. This is usually a year during which children who are five years of age begin their public school experience. Kindergarten is viewed by the lay public and others as a bridge between the nursery school as play/socialization and first grade as the serious business of learning to read by means of basal readers and workbooks. All states support kindergarten education, although only eight states mandate attendance.[1]

More than 3 million children, 90 percent of the children in the United States, attend kindergarten.[2] Twenty-five percent of these children come from impoverished homes.[3] Demographers predict that before the end of this century, children who grew up in poverty will constitute a significant portion of the population of the United States.[4] At the same time, increasing cultural diversity and changing work patterns, with varied definitions of what constitutes a family, suggest that school, particularly kindergarten, may be one of the most stable, nurturant features in the lives of many children. This being the case, there is a need to develop kindergarten programs that are both culturally sensitive and intellectually stimulating.

Recent discussions of kindergarten have gone beyond current circumstances to consideration of matching the acts of teaching more closely to the conditions under which kindergarten children learn best. Increasingly, these discussions focus on developmentally appropriate content and methods for kindergarten that are distinctly different from curricular and instructional practices of the primary school.[5] There is concern among early childhood educators and developmental specialists about "hothousing" or pressuring young children by a heavy reliance on workbooks and other paper-and-pencil activities, thus robbing children of time for experiential learning and, perhaps, creating behavior problems.[6]

These discussions highlight a fundamental disagreement among educators about early childhood programs in public schools. This difference of opinion is most clearly seen through analysis of current curriculum, policy and staffing, and administrative practice regarding kindergarten.

ORIENTATION OF CURRICULUM AND METHOD

The questions we ask about programs propel how they are represented, where they go, and how time and space are used. Dewey suggested that it is worthwhile for teachers to help children move toward the funded knowledge of humanity in ways that are consistent with their present modes of development.[7] Whitehead made the distinction between information, knowledge, and wisdom, and recommended that wisdom—the use of knowledge—be the ultimate aim of education.[8]

Society expects kindergartens to prepare future adults who can adapt effectively to a complex and unpredictable world. Research on kindergarten and early childhood education should help kindergarten teachers and administrators in this work. Many kindergarten studies, however, lack reference to classroom organization and curriculum content. Some have looked at attitudes of parents and teachers. Most studies note that teachers in half-day programs feel rushed. Few studies focus on attitudes of children, although there is increasing study of social competence.[9]

What is emerging in the kindergarten field is a variety of paradigms for kindergarten programming, which grow out of significantly different views of what is developmentally appropriate, how learning takes place, and what teaching is worthwhile. In recent years, kindergartens have become more academic/formal and less intellectual/experiential. While both academic/formal and intellectual/experiential programs show improved test scores, school boards that are considering whether to extend the kindergarten day need to be aware that they are likely to extend whatever curriculum is already being offered. There are considerations that suggest that school districts with academic/formal programs should reexamine their curriculum, rather than extend the day.

The academic/formal view is largely behavioristic: The young learner is seen as a reactor to external stimuli and the subject of study is teaching. The intellectual/experiential view is largely constructivistic: The young learner is seen as an interpreter of interactions and the subject of study is how children learn. This perspective acknowledges that young children's perception of the world differs from that of adults. The intellectual/experiential orientation also subsumes developmentally and socially oriented approaches and integrates play as one of six conditions of learning. (The other five are inductive experiences, cognitive dissonance, social interaction, physical experiences, and competence.[10])

Constance Kamii points out that much that is behavioristic is subsumed under constructivist theory, but the process is not reversible.[11] The academic/formal approach assumes that all children who are exposed to the same stimuli at the same time take away the same learning. There is a fallacy in this thinking. In actual fact, each child processes information differently and is likely to learn more with varied approaches.

Figure 1 compares the emphases of the academic/formal kindergarten (in which children are expected to adapt to the school's teaching procedures) with the intellectual/experiential program (in which the school adapts to the child's strategies for learning).

Figure 1.   A Comparison of Predominant Conditions of Learning in Academic and Intellectual Kindergartens

Academic Kindergarten	Intellectual Kindergarten
children adapt	school adapts
child as passive	child as active
child as dependent	child as autonomous
whole-group instruction	small-group and individual instruction
individual tasks	balanced small-group cooperative and individual tasks
preset material is covered	children's capacity to learn is extended
3Rs instructional focus	concepts and applied skills
separate subjects	integrated subjects
workbooks	concrete materials and quality literature
verbal, informational emphasis	constructivist, problem-solving emphasis
single correct answers	alternative solutions generated
work and play divided	play is one condition of learning
holiday rituals marked	multicultural content based on the study of social experience

While most young children trust, and want to please, their teachers, the most creative children are likely not to conform to the demands of academic programs, by doing things differently from the majority way,[12] or, alternatively, leaving situations through their capacity for fantasy.[13] These children, who are merely engaging in age-appropriate behavior, are often labeled emotionally disturbed and referred to psychologists. They can work more easily in adaptive classrooms where small-group interactions predominate and where responsible behavior is expected. These considerations influence the cost of education as well as express ethical concerns.

Schools confront a moral dilemma because many children can perform the verbal tricks for which they are trained in rote-learning encounters. The workbook phenomenon in particular is in my opinion a form of sanctioned child abuse in early childhood education. Sixty-five-month-old children are expected to sit for hours and fill in workbooks that repeatedly test them. Even though children can perform in these ways, it is immoral to require that they do so, because the practice is so contrary to what we know about child development and learning. It is therefore essential to make explicit what one considers to be worthwhile learning, the nature of knowledge, and what kinds of human beings a society values.

Schools traditionally have been the single institution in society most directly charged with the task of extending the intellectual development of children. However, the most benevolent, warm-spirited, well-intentioned teacher cannot shield a child from failure unless that individual adapts teaching to the child's ways of learning and developmental level. Such a practice leads to educational equity, empowerment, and responsibility.

EDUCATIONAL EQUITY, EMPOWERMENT, AND RESPONSIBILITY

How schools deal with equity issues is a reflection of their orientation toward academic/formal or intellectual/experiential curriculum and methods. In schools where the academic/formal perspective predominates, those children who are assessed as less able to succeed in school tend to come from low-income and culturally varied groups. Those children are usually given rote tasks to do and are asked to respond to recall questions.[14] In contrast, more successful children are more often engaged in creative tasks and are asked to respond to questions that call for analysis, evaluation, and synthesis.

Empowerment is another important issue that arises from the differences between the organization of the academic/formal and the intellectual/experiential classroom structures. Empowerment refers to children's sense of their power to direct their own learning. Anthropologists Frederick Erickson and Gerald Mohatt described two teachers, one (I) who accommodated to children's learning paces and styles and the other (II) who expected them to accommodate to his directives.[15] Teacher II created sharp boundaries between work and play. Work was the area of teacher control. In contrast, Teacher I did not separate work and play as sharply, adapted to children's rhythms as a way to gauge the time for new activities, and paced the same tasks more gradually. Nevertheless, children in both classrooms spent the same amount of time engaged in subject matter. In Teacher I's classroom, children were seated at table groupings whereas in Teacher II's they were seated individually in rows and spent more time in whole-group instruction. While both teachers circulated among the students, Teacher I addressed comments to small groups and individuals "privately," part of the children's cultural "etiquette" that avoided overt and direct social control. Teacher II, even when working with small groups, would put people in the "spotlight" by addressing them "publicly" across the room. Teacher I accommodated to the children's culture, creating a more culturally sensitive classroom. Teacher II intuitively limited children's interactions with one another. That teacher focused on the children's need to adapt to the group.

Part of what is at issue in consideration of both equity and empowerment is the question of how to help children assume responsibility for their own actions, including their learning and various forms of self-regulation. Based on understandings of social organization within schools, anthropologist Sylvia Hart has suggested that schools might group children according to substantive interest or motivation rather than only the ability to perform on linear tests.[16]

Intellectually oriented teachers regularly provide children with choices from among learning activities that use social interaction as a strength. Thus, a child who may be viewed as disruptive in the academic setting can be viewed as capable in the intellectual kindergarten. The power to choose among activities and between social interaction and privacy stimulates self-direction and responsible attention to tasks.

Children in an intellectual setting have more of a sense of personal power and take more responsibility for their own behavior when they have opportunities to engage in activity that is appropriate. With guidance, they are expected to pace themselves, select from among varied activities, and set problems for themselves and others. They have motives for applying the three Rs to meaningful content. In the pursuit of such choices, they acquire additional autonomy and wisdom. This approach provides a long-term commitment to scholarship. If, on the other hand, the appeal is solely to the authority of the school for the teacher and the teacher for the child, it becomes especially difficult to teach children to say no to damaging influences in their lives, such as child abusers, and to peer-group pressures for drugs and group vandalism.

POLICIES AFFECTING CURRENT TRENDS

Although state policies affecting kindergarten are diverse, there is a remarkable uniformity of curricular trends across the nation. In numerous settings, kindergarten programs reflect both the effects of international economic competition and the changing family structure in American society. With pressure on schools to accomplish more earlier and to provide child-care services in addition to education, kindergartens have been forced to adapt. The extension of public kindergarten education into new parts of the country during the past fifteen years is one manifestation of those influences. In addition, traditional half-day programs have been lengthened so that twenty-two states now support local varieties of extended-day and all-day kindergarten programs, compared with one state in 1974.[17]

Local school districts, sometimes within broad state guidelines, control kindergarten curricula and, despite teacher certification policies, also decide who will teach kindergarten.

TEACHER CERTIFICATION POLICIES

Public policy concerning early childhood teacher certification is ragged and inadequate, despite findings by researchers that teacher training in early childhood education and child development were significant factors in children's school achievement.[18] Specially designated early childhood teacher preparation requirements may be as little as two courses or as much as a master's degree plus teaching experience.* Thirty-six states have some provision for certifying or endorsing (an alternative strand within the elementary school license) kindergarten teachers.

Table 1 charts teacher certification for early childhood education in the United States. Fifteen states and the District of Columbia provide for certification; twenty-one endorse kindergarten specialties within the general elementary certificate; and fourteen have no unique regulation of kindergarten teachers. Thus, it is common practice for upper-elementary teachers or others without preparation in early childhood to work in kindergarten. The situation is critical because the demand on educational services for young children is expanding. Public policies are needed that more vigorously support certification of whose who will teach young children. Administrative policies, too, should become more supportive of an early childhood perspective that leans more toward the intellectual/experiential and away from the academic/formal.

ADMINISTRATIVE PRACTICES REGARDING KINDERGARTEN

Current administrative practice toward kindergarten places stress on academic readiness with a new set of "three Rs" — readiness testing, "redshirting," and retention.

Readiness Testing

Prescreening tests are currently used to determine children's readiness for academic work. Children who do not pass the tests may be excluded or placed in a junior kindergarten. In contrast to these uses by elementary school administrators and teachers, early childhood educators would like readiness tests to be used diagnostically to consider children's social competence; emotional, physical, and cognitive learning; or cultural development.

The debate over readiness testing has become so heated as to lead to a "call for a moratorium on the use of achievement tests in grades K–2."[19]

---

*Inasmuch as there is ongoing change in state certification, individual situations may be altered by the time this appears in print.

Table 1.   Teacher Certification for Early Childhood Education in the United States

State	N	Pre-K	K	1	2	3	4	Sp-Ed	None
Alabama	+	+	+	+	+	+			
Alaska	+	E +	E +	+	+	+			
Arizona									—
Arkansas		E	E	(only at Master's Degree)					
California		E	E	E	E	E			
Colorado	E	E	E	E	E	E			
Connecticut	E	E	E	E	E	E			
Delaware	+	+	+	+	+	+			
Florida	E	E	E	E	E	E			
Georgia	E	E	E	E	E	E			
Hawaii									—
Idaho			E						
Illinois	E	E	E	E	E	E			
Indiana			+	+	+	+			
Iowa		E	E						
Kansas		E	E						
Kentucky			E	E	E	E	E		
Louisiana	E	E	E						
Maine									—
Maryland	+	+	+	+	+				
Massachusetts	+	+	+	+	+				
Michigan									—
Minnesota			E						
Mississippi									—
Missouri	+	+	+	+	+	+			
Montana									—
Nebraska	E	E	E	E	E	E			
Nevada								E, 0–4 yrs.	
New Hampshire									—
New Jersey		+	+						
New Mexico									—
New York									—
North Carolina			E	E	E	E	E		
North Dakota			E						
Ohio		+	+						
Oklahoma	+	+	+						
Oregon									—
Pennsylvania	+	+	+	+	+	+			
Rhode Island	+	+	+	+	+				

Table 1.   Teacher Certification for Early Childhood Education in the United States (Continued)

State	N	Pre-K	K	1	2	3	4	Sp-Ed	None
South Carolina			+	+	+	+			
South Dakota	E	E							
Tennessee			+	+	+	+			
Texas	E	E	E	E	E	E			
Utah	E	E	E	E	E	E			
Vermont	E	E	E	E	E	E			
Virginia	+	+	+	+	+	+			—
Washington									
Washington, DC		+	+						
West Virginia	E	E	E	E	E	E	E		
Wisconsin	+	+	+						
Wyoming									—

E = Endorsement on elementary certification; + = Certification

Redshirting

Consistent with readiness testing, "redshirting"† — the process of keeping children out of school for an additional year — is a growing trend. Parents of children — especially boys — who are close to the cutoff date for admission to kindergarten, responding to documentation about younger boys' having more trouble in school, have redshirted their own children. Redshirting reflects parental fears of the children's repeating a year at school, as well as their desire for their children to do well and achieve high scores in an academic setting. As with the varied expectations for readiness tests, redshirting reflects the differences in expectations among primary/elementary educators and early childhood educators.

October seems to be a common cut-off date for kindergarten admission, although variations between June 1 and December 1 exist. Some school districts have followed private school practice and raised the age of admission. Nevertheless, admission decisions need to account for the fact that there will still be a one-year difference between the oldest and the youngest children in a class.

Retention

At the completion of the kindergarten year, children who do not master the skills expected in an academic first grade might repeat kindergarten or be placed in a junior first grade. There has been a considerable body of research about the effects of such retention on children. Asa Hilliard III makes the

†Redshirting is a term derived from football policies, according to Ralph Frick, "In Support of Academic Redshirting," *Young Children* 41 (1986): 9–10.

point that this practice places "inordinate stress" on low-income and culturally varied children, who feel culpable even though the school setting is to blame.[20] Indeed, he and others note that grade retention lowers aspiration levels and performance on tests, and adversely affects social behavior,[21] thus undermining the child's self-esteem — an important factor in academic performance.[22] Findings that socially promoted younger children,[23] or children who were low achievers, did better academically and socially than retained children[24] suggest that retention for academic reasons alone may be counterproductive. Here again is an issue on which the opinions of early childhood educators and elementary educators are at odds.

The three Rs of readiness testing, redshirting, and retention reflect a trend toward practices that are not based on either theory or research about how children learn. Even with training, many early childhood teachers feel overwhelmed by institutional pressures that include administrators who do not have an understanding of developmentally appropriate programs. Teachers with specialized preparation in early education report that although they do not believe that workbooks or lockstep methods are worthwhile, they feel compelled by administrative or parental pressure to use practices that are in conflict with their philosophies and what they know about child development, learning, and teaching. J. Amos Hatch and Evelyn B. Freeman have documented this situation in Ohio,[25] but this "academic bootcamp"[26] is present across the country.[27]

With the power to make curriculum decisions comes the power to take responsibility. In-service teachers need to extend their own opportunities for professionalism, a process that is beginning politically and one that needs to be extended substantively as well. Collaborative and inductive learning conditions must be made available to practicing teachers. They need collegial planning time and school support for the self-reflective study of teaching, using personal teaching data and coaching by colleagues.[28]

Although I have discussed the polarities of the academic and intellectual kindergartens, and although the academic forms have been proliferating, *it is inaccurate to assume that truly intellectual education has been tried and been passed over.* It is, however, accurate to say that the academic model for young children has been used widely and has been found wanting. The problem of school failure for many inner-city, low-income, and culturally diverse groups continues. These children feel discouraged and learn to perceive the school as alien.

While children are resilient and often can conform to academic demands, educators and policymakers need to consider that the intellectual kindergarten can subsume many of the expected accomplishments of the academic scope and exceed that scope.

EPILOGUE: CHALLENGES FOR PRIMARY EDUCATION

It is time for reform in primary education to reflect the best of early child-hood practices. The school process in first grade has been essentially the same during the past two decades.[29] Much existing primary practice is culturally insufficient and sterile.

Articulation between exemplary kindergarten practices and first grades can help to maintain and extend educational opportunities for children who come from diverse socioeconomic and cultural heritages. This would include extending the use of culturally rich learning centers in which children can practice independence, responsibility, and self-pacing. It would also include organizing small-group and individual instruction. Schools need to help children to relate school activities and projects to their personal rates of learning, motives, and extended community experiences. Developmentally appropriate *content* needs to be the center of curriculum with *skills applied* to the pursuit of knowledge and wisdom.

Therefore, there is a need for site-specific curriculum development. This means that school systems would move away from district-wide adoptions of texts to unique building-level decision making and the collegial involvement of kindergarten and primary teachers in planning curriculum. In turn, principals need to have an understanding of developmentally appropriate curriculum for young children. They also need skills in working collaboratively with autonomous professional teachers. State education departments should legislate relevant professional early childhood teacher certification throughout the United States. Teacher-association campaigns for teacher empowerment in curriculum development also should support early childhood teacher certification.

There is a need for collaborative interdisciplinary research with teachers in classrooms. Universities, professional organizations, and public policy agents ought to support the documentation and sharing of research findings that have implications for teachers' use. Support for longitudinal studies is particularly relevant. The fundamental disagreement among educators about early childhood programs in public schools will probably not be resolved until such research is conducted, implications are drawn for practice, and those implications are translated into policy regarding teacher certification and licensure. Until then, the "miseducation" of young children is likely to continue.[30] If we do not address this situation now, when will we? If we do not do it, who will?

Notes

1   Sandra Longfellow Robinson, "Kindergarten in America: Five Major Trends," *Phi Delta Kappan* 68 (1987): 529–30; and Lorrie A. Shepard and Mary Lee Smith, "Synthesis of Research on School Readiness and Kindergarten Retention," *Educational Leadership* 44 (1986): 79.

2   Bernard Spodek, "Kindergarten," *The International Encyclopedia of Education: Research and Studies*, vol. 5, ed. Torsten Husen and T. Nevil Postlethwaite (New York: Pergamon, 1985), pp. 2812–14.

3   Robert Halpern, "Major Social and Demographic Trends Affecting Young Families: Implications for Early Childhood Care and Education," *Young Children* 42 (1987): 34.

4   Harold Hodgkinson, "The Right Schools for the Right Kids," *Educational Leadership* 45 (1988): 10–14.

5   International Reading Association, Early Childhood and Literacy Development Committee, "Literacy Development and Pre-First Grade," *Childhood Education* 63 (1986): 110–11; Sue Bredekamp, ed., *Developmentally Appropriate Practice* (Washington, D.C.: National Association for the Education of Young Children, 1986); Joan Moyer, Harriet A. Egertson, and Joan Isenberg, "Association for Childhood Education International Position Paper: The Child-Centered Kindergarten," *Childhood Education* 63 (1987): 235–42; and National Association for the Education of Young Children, "NAEYC Position Statement on Standardized Testing of Young Children 3 Through 8 Years of Age," *Young Children* 43 (1988): 42–47.

6   *Arithmetic Teacher*, February 1988; Patricia Minuchin, "Schools, Families, and the Development of Young Children," *Early Childhood Research Quarterly* 2 (1987): 247; and Irving E. Sigel, "Does Hothousing Rob Children of Their Childhood?" *Early Childhood Research Quarterly* 2 (1987): 223.

7   John Dewey, *Democracy and Education* (New York: Macmillan, 1961), p. 184.

8   Alfred North Whitehead, *The Aims of Education* (New York: Mentor, 1929), pp. 41, 43.

9   Dominic P. Gullo et al., "A Comparative Study of 'All-Day,' 'Alternate-Day,' and 'Half-Day' Kindergarten Schedules: Effects on Achievement and Classroom Social Behaviors," *Journal of Research in Childhood Education* 1 (1986): 87–94; Jack W. Humphreys, *A Longitudinal Study of the Consequences of Full Day Kindergarten* (Evansville, Ind.: Evansville-Vanderburgh School Corp., 1988); and Vincent T. Puleo, "A Review and Critique of Research on Full-Day Kindergarten," *Elementary School Journal* 88 (1988): 427–39.

10   Doris Pronin Fromberg, *The Full-Day Kindergarten* (New York: Teachers College Press, 1987).

11   Constance Kamii, "Piaget's Theory, Behaviorism, and Other Theories of Education," *Journal of Education* 161 (1979): 13–33.

12   Shirley Brice Heath, *Ways with Words: Language, Life, and Work in Communities and Classrooms* (Cambridge: Cambridge University Press, 1983); and E. Paul Torrance, *Rewarding Creative Talent* (Englewood Cliffs, N.J.: Prentice-Hall, 1965).

13   Jerome Singer and Dorothy Singer, "The Values of Imagination," in *Play and Learning*, ed. Brian Sutton-Smith (New York: Gardner, 1979), p. 199.

14   Carl Bereiter and Siegfried Engelman, *Teaching the Disadvantaged Child in the Preschool* (Englewood Cliffs, N.J.: Prentice-Hall, 1967); Sylvia Hart, "Analyzing the Social Organization for Reading in One Elementary School," in *Doing the Ethnography of Schooling*, ed. George Spindler (New York: Holt, Rinehart & Winston, 1982), pp. 410–38; Heath, *Ways with Words*; and idem, "Questioning at Home and at School: A Comparative Study," in *Doing the Ethnography of Schooling*, pp. 102–31.

15   Frederick Erickson and Gerald Mohatt, "Cultural Organization or Participation Structures in Two Classrooms of Indian Students," in *Doing the Ethnography of Schooling*, pp. 132–74.

16   Hart, "Analyzing the Social Organization for Reading," p. 436.

17   Robinson, "Kindergarten in America," p. 530.

18   Richard Ruopp et al., *Children at the Center: Summary Findings and Their Implications* (Cambridge, Mass.: Abt, 1979), p. 98; Lawrence J. Schweinhart, Jeffrey J. Koshel, and Anne Bridgman, "Policy Options for Preschool Programs," *Phi Delta Kappan* 68 (1987): 527; and Cynthia Warger, ed. *A Resource Guide to Public School Early Childhood Programs* (Alexandria, Va.: Association for Supervision and Curriculum Development, 1988), p. 112.

19   Constance Kamii, ed., *Achievement Tests in Early Childhood Education: Power in Need of Accountability* (Washington, D.C.: National Association for the Education of Young Children, forthcoming).

20   Asa G. Hilliard III, "What Is Quality Child Care?" in *What Is Quality Child Care?*, ed. Bettye M. Caldwell and Asa G. Hilliard III (Washington, D.C.: National Association for the Education of Young Children, 1985), pp. 17–32.

21   Ibid.; Diane L. Plummer, Marylin Hazzard Lineberger, and William G. Graziano, "The Academic and Social Consequences of Grade Retention: A Convergent Analysis," in *Current Topics in Early Childhood Education*, vol. 6, ed. Lilian G. Katz (Norwood, N.J.: Ablex, 1986), pp. 224–52; Shepard and Smith, "Synthesis of Research on School Readiness"; and Lorrie R. Skarpness and David K. Carson, "Correlates of Kindergarten Adjustment: Temperament and Communicative Competence," *Early Childhood Research Quarterly* 2 (1987): 367–76.

22   Prescott Lecky, *Theory of Self-Consistency* (Garden City, N.Y.: Doubleday, 1969).

23   E. Milling Kinard and Helen Reinherz, "Birthdate Effects on School Performance and Adjustment: A Longitudinal Study," *Journal of Educational Research* 79 (1986): 366–72.

24   Shepard and Smith, "Synthesis of Research on School Readiness and Kindergarten Retention"; and idem, "Effects of Kindergarten Retention at the End of First Grade," *Psychology in the Schools* 24 (1987): 346–57.

25   J. Amos Hatch and Evelyn B. Freeman, "Ohio Kindergarten Programs: Perspectives of Teachers, Principals, and Supervisors" (Paper presented at the annual meeting of the American Educational Research Association, Washington, D.C., April 1987).

26   Christine M. L. Roberts, "Whatever Happened to Kindergarten?" *Educational Leadership* 44 (1986): 34.

27   Nancy K. Carver, "Reading Readiness: Aspects Overlooked in Structured Readiness Programs and Workbooks," *Childhood Education* 62 (1986): 256–69; Dolores Durkin, "A Classroom-Observation Study of Reading Instruction in Kindergarten," *Early Childhood Research Quarterly* 2 (1987): 284, 288; Harriet A. Egertson, "Recapturing Kindergarten for 5-Year-Olds," *Education Week*, May 20, 1987, pp. 27–28, 19; David Elkind, "Formal Education and Early Childhood Education: An Essential Difference," *Phi Delta Kappan* 67 (1986): 631–36; Suzi Nall, "Bridging the Gap: Preschool to Kindergarten," *Childhood Education* 59 (1982): 107–10; Samuel G. Sava, "Development, Not Academics," *Young Children* 42 (1987): 15; Janet Stone, "Early Childhood Mathematics: Make It Manipulative!" *Young Children* 42 (1987): 16–23; and Connie K. Williams and Constance Kamii, "How Do Children Learn by Handling Objects?" *Young Children* 42 (1986): 23–26.

28   Jerome Bruner, *Under Five in Britian* (Ypsilani, Mich.: High/Scope, 1980); G. Thomas Fox, Jr., et al., *Collaboration: Lessons Learned from Experience* (Washington, D.C.: American Association of Colleges for Teacher Education, 1986); David W. Johnson and Robert T. Johnson, "Research Shows the Benefits of Adult Cooperation," *Educational Leadership* 45 (1987): 27–30; Bruce Joyce and Beverly Showers, "The Coaching of Teaching," *Educational Leadership* 40 (1982): 4–10; and Ann Lieberman, "Collaborative Research: Working With, Not Working On . . .," *Educational Leadership* 42 (1986): 28–32.

29   Doris R. Entwisle et al., "The Schooling Process in First Grade: Two Samples a Decade Apart," *American Educational Research Journal* 23 (1986): 587–613.

30   David Elkind, *Miseducation: Preschoolers at Risk* (New York: Alfred Knopf, 1987).

A Comprehensive Model for Integrating Child Care and Early Childhood Education

BETTYE M. CALDWELL
University of Arkansas

Arguing that we need to fully integrate child care and early childhood education, Caldwell traces some of the roots and consequences of their separation in America. She describes her own establishment of a "day care school" and urges adoption of the term educare *to signal the intimate connections of education and care that we need as a national policy for our children.*

It is gratifying that the editors of this issue of the *Teachers College Record* chose to identify it as concerned with early childhood education and child care. The conjunction "and" in that phrase is the good news. The bad news is that a conjunction is needed at all, for the two halves of the phrase actually represent one service — a comprehensive program for young children that may be utilized for varying lengths of time during a day, a week, a year, or several years.

The persistence of the myth that early childhood education and child care are different services represents an interesting exercise in conceptual deception. Perhaps as much as anything else, this has been due to semantic status factors. Just as it is more fashionable to say that your adult child is a "university student" than to say that he or she "goes to college," it is clearly more socially acceptable to have a child in an early childhood education program than it is in child care or, heaven forbid, day care! For your selection of the former type of program, you are likely to be praised for being a conscientious parent. If you opt for the latter, you are sure to be suspected of neglect and lack of concern.

HISTORICAL ANTECEDENTS OF THE FALSE SCHISM

There are legitimate historical reasons for the customary division of early childhood services into education and child care. Each of these arose from a different source and, along the way, acquired a host of descriptors that appeared to distinguish it sharply from the other. The two types of service were even described as meeting different needs. Some of these historical distinctions are highlighted in Table 1.

Table 1. Market Segmentation of Early Childhood Programs into "Education" and "Child Care"

Early Childhood Education	Child Care
CHARACTERISTIC DESCRIPTORS	
Is an educational service	Is a social welfare program
Essentially for the middle class and affluent	Established to serve lower-class and poor children
A service for intact families	A service for pathological families
Operates in a school or center	Occurs in an institution
Is mainly a service for children	Is mainly a service for parents
Is a supplement to home care	Is substitute care—or worse, custodial care
Is privately funded	Is publicly funded
Operates only a few hours a day	Enrolls children for long hours every day
HUMAN NEEDS SERVED	
Provides education and training—enriches the lives of children	Provides care and protection—keeps children from harming others and themselves (starting fires, having accidents)
Encourages value choice and decision making	Imposes values and instills behavior patterns
Encourages freedom and accepts diversity	Imposes conformity
Serves as a family support	Weakens the family
Democratizes children	"Sovietizes" children

From the table it is clear that most of the socially acceptable descriptors belonged to early childhood education. Taken as a whole, these descriptors make it clear that this was a service designed for "normal" children from intact, middle-class families with enough economic resources to pay for a service not considered essential enough by society at large to have been provided as a free and universally available public service. It was an extra in the lives of the children, something that perhaps only a few children would experience. Although high-quality programs offered tips for parents on how to meet the needs of their children, this activity was but an auxiliary to the service provided the children themselves. The heart of the curriculum was the social development of the children, many of whom could be expected to come from small families offering few opportunities for extensive interaction with other children of similar ages. Since the program operated for only a few hours each day, possibly for only two or three days a week, the educational activities did not seriously alter the pattern and type of child rearing the child was receiving at home.

Not so with the poor relation, day care. It had a different clientele. Children in attendance were mainly poor, and their families could be considered as showing one or another type of social pathology, such as a home broken by death or divorce and then managed by a mother who was mentally or physically ill, incompetent, or simply unavailable because she worked outside the home. The children's program was really as much or more a service for the mothers as it was for the children. It kept the children off the street and out of trouble. It substituted for the mother rather than supplementing her care, as was the case with its rich (by comparison) cousin. The care provided was often called "custodial" or "institutional" and was sharply differentiated from the type of care children received at home. A major aim of the activities made available to the children was to teach them how to behave properly and to eliminate from their repertoire behaviors that were not socially acceptable. The children were expected to conform to what was expected of them, not to express their individuality.

These differences in program characteristics had distinct political overtones, even though the field itself was largely ignored as an area for major social policy until fairly recently. The type of program offered in early childhood education, with its emphasis on free choice of activity and individuality of expression, was completely consistent with democratic ideals. It could be described as "democratizing" children. Day care, on the other hand, through the imposition of a set of values consonant with program sponsorship, public or private, and its emphasis on group goals and activities seemed more akin to "communal" upbringing. Although the accusation did not appear until the fairly recent past of child care, fears were expressed that it would "sovietize" American children. Any service that offered even the most remote possibility of such an achievement was doomed to disfavor in America. So, by and large, has it been with the child-care field until fairly recently.

The reality of these distinctions is forcibly emphasized in the following definition of day care found in one of the most influential and widely used references of its day, the 1960 edition of the Child Welfare League of America's *Standards for Day Care Service*:

> Day-care service has to be differentiated from nursery school or kindergarten, and from extended school services and other programs for

school-age children offered as part of elementary school systems. These have education of young children as their main purpose. The primary purpose of a day-care service is the care and protection of children. This purpose, the reasons for which a child and family may need it, and the responsibility shared with parents distinguish a day-care service from educational programs.[1]

This carefully formulated definition, prepared by a social welfare rather than an educational organization, serves as a reminder of perhaps the most likely explanation of why a schism developed: Services that were identified by the two different labels were provided under different auspices and thus comprised two distinct turfs. Turfs, once established, have to be guarded by both semantic and programmatic manipulations. So has it been throughout much of this century—the time during which both variants have had any important impact on the domain of human service. At this juncture in history, however, the two turfs are becoming one large greensward.

THE MOVE TOWARD ECUMENISM

My schismatic metaphor in this narrative implies that there was once a truly integrated concept of what an early childhood program should be. There was, but it never had much credence in America. Montessori's original project in Rome[2] and the plans of Robert Owen in Scotland[3] represent perfect examples of the integration of educational and social welfare models and objectives. Montessori candidly stated that she wanted to keep the young children off the street and out of the halls of the tenements, but she also wanted to educate them according to the methods she had learned from Seguin and then improved on her own. For some reason, however, as the Montessori movement, along with other European ideas such as those of the McMillan sisters,[4] crossed the Atlantic, it became narrow and more limited in scope. Programs became curricula, and anything that approximated a coherent set of ways of organizing teaching experiences for young children became identified as belonging in the domain of education.

The schism that soon developed on this side of the Atlantic was not settled by a Council of Constance. Nor did it heal as the result of persistent and perhaps frenzied campaigning and evangelizing on the subject.[5] Rather it is closing slowly but inexorably, and with no major visible scars, as a result of changes in the demographics of modern family life. In fact, these changes are occurring so rapidly that statistics chronicling them are almost obsolete before they appear in print. According to data released in 1987 by the U.S. Bureau of the Census, 57 percent of mothers whose youngest child is under six are in the labor force.[6] This represents a 69 percent increase between 1970 and 1985. Simple extrapolation of such trends suggests that, by the end of the century just a decade from now, we can expect 90 percent of mothers of young children — virtually all who are physically and mentally competent — to be in the labor force.

This demographic reality forces an end to either a doctrinal or auspicial schism relating to early childhood programs. No matter how much the parents of the almost 9 million children younger than five who are in child care[7] in America might want their children to participate in a high-status early childhood education program, their need for longer term, high-quality "care and protection" for their young children will take precedence. Though professionals representing both services may have resisted ecumenism for their own historical reasons, today's parents are saying "Get your act together. We don't want and won't accept just part of it." To labor the biblical metaphor just one more time, they are saying, as Laban did to Jacob when he came to wed his younger daughter, "If you want Rachel, you've got to take Leah first."

ADVANTAGES OF AN INTEGRATED SERVICE

There are many advantages to both consumers and providers of a comprehensive child development program that incorporates the best — and eliminates the worst — of traditional child care and education. One way to illustrate some of these is to describe the Kramer Project in Little Rock, Arkansas, which I had the privilege to develop and direct from 1969 to 1978.[8]

THE KRAMER PROJECT

The project involved conversion of a regular public elementary school with three vacant classrooms into a day-care school.[9] Continuity between the early childhood years and whatever developmental intervention was available then and the subsequent educational histories of the middle childhood period was a major goal of the project. However, that vertical aspect of program integration achieved at Kramer is less relevant for this article than the horizontal integration — the fusion of child care and education into one comprehensive service. The programmatic conversion was surprisingly easy, despite the semantic resistance to a new label that would accurately describe the model.

The school officially opened at 6:45 A.M. and closed at 6:00 P.M. year round. However, only about two-thirds of the children in the school attended any longer than they would have if the child-care program had not been available. The child care was available to all the children enrolled in the school, not just the very young ones. The actual age range was from six months to twelve years. In general, however, there were few children older than ten who participated in child care during the regular school year. During the summer, when there was little for them to do in their neighborhoods, children right up to the sixth-grade level tended to enroll.[10] Children arrived in a steady stream from the opening moment onward, and they departed in roughly the same sequence in the afternoon. About fifty children would be at Kramer by 7:30, and another one hundred arrived between 7:30 and 8:30, when the regular classes began. In the afternoon, peak departure times would be at 4:00 and again at 5:00, with only about thirty children still at school at the 6:00 closing time. The summer program operated on the same hours, but there were never as many children enrolled during the summer. Older siblings were often utilized for child care during that time.

The extra hours were staffed by part-time and split-time personnel, or, for the early childhood segment, by staggered work schedules that covered the full day. This was necessary in order to conform to the Arkansas regulation that at least one certified teacher be on the premises any time there were children in the building. It proved to be a surprisingly compatible arrangement with personal and family timetables. Traditionally teachers must report to work very early; yet there are always some who are "late" persons who do not like to go to work at the crack of dawn. At Kramer it was rare for the full day not to be covered with volunteer time choices. The same was true for the summer program. Many elementary teachers would like to work during the summer in order to earn extra income but cannot find jobs. If more wanted to work than were needed to cover the number of children enrolled, we arranged for teams to split the time and to share the jobs.

THE EXTENDED-DAY PROGRAM

At the outset of the project, we overloaded the extended hours (and the summer months) with academic and remedial work. Kramer served an economically disadvantaged population, and many of the children needed extra academic hours and creative enrichment activities. After the first year we modified this considerably, especially during the afternoon hours. Although we had thought this would be a good time to do homework or to participate in programmed learning activities, by and large this was not the case. The children were tired and needed a change of pace. Accordingly, from the second year onward, late-day activities offered a choice from two main categories: sports/games/gymnastics and art/music. The sports program may not have left a lasting impression, but evidence of the art activities still abounds. Over the years the children painted murals in the halls, game lines on the playground, props for various stage productions, and one another. They loved it.

PARENTAL REACTIONS

In a critique of the value of this kind of integrated child care and education service, reaction of the parents cannot be overlooked. The Kramer parents were the most passionate supporters of the idea and were the most vocal when it became necessary to move the program out of Kramer, even though most components of the program were being preserved.[11] Incidentally, it was always difficult for the Kramer parents to understand that many leaders in the fields of both education and day care were opposed to this combination of the two types of service. The more articulate ones would say, "But that's the way it should always be."

Although we all liked to think that this endorsement was primarily due to the high-quality program, it was probably related more to sheer convenience than anything else. Kramer was centrally located, and dropping off children on the way to work was fairly easy. Of even greater value to the parents was the fact that any and all of their young children could receive extended day care there. At the time Kramer was established, child care for children younger than three was rarely available in the same facility that cared for children in the three-to-six age range. Certainly none of those facilities also cared for and educated elementary children who were too young to remain at home alone either after the parents left in the morning or before they returned in the afternoon. There was something of value for all of them at Kramer.

THE SERVICE IS *EDUCARE*

Our experiences at Kramer, plus years of exposure to the hyprocisy involved in declarations that child care and education are different services, have led me to urge the adoption of the word *educare* to describe this integrated service. It is a word whose time has come. It should be written without a hyphen and without capitalization. It is the Latin word for "educate," which, in the literal sense, means "to lead out of," but in our modern ignorance of Latin roots few people will know that. What is more important is that it effectively combines "education" and "care" into a single word and thus promises an integrated service that will augment parental care and foster the development of young children.

I began using this term over twenty years ago, when I first became conscious of the pernicious implications of the false dichotomy between education and care. However, on learning that a private for-profit chain used the term as a corporate name, I abandoned my quest to have others adopt it. However, as is often the case when a good idea comes along, more than one person is likely to have it at about the same time. Dorothy Hewes, who had used it verbally from about 1970, used it in a textbook written with Barbara Hartman in 1972.[12] Magda Gerber has used a related term in her organization, Resources for Infant Educaring. Groups in several countries (Malaysia, South Africa) use the term consistently, and others (such as New Zealand) are considering adopting it. It appears that the logic of the term—plus dissatisfaction with the semantic confusion that now surrounds the field—is beginning to gain adherents.

CHALLENGES TO BE OVERCOME

The rosy picture painted above about the integrated educare service provided at Kramer School should not be interpreted as indicating that there are no problems associated with trying to develop such a program. There were plenty twenty years ago, and there are plenty today. In essence, most of the problems stem from the fact that people primarily associated with or supportive of either traditional early childhood education or traditional child care do not trust those primarily associated with the other.

MISTRUST OF CHILD CARE

For many years, mistrust of and hostility toward child care appeared to be stronger than negative attitudes in the reverse direction. Many early childhood educators who correctly interpreted the demographic trends and saw the pressing need for more child care legitimately feared that an expansion of the service that was already there would be inimical to the welfare of children and destroy the credibility of other early childhood programs. Just letting child care as it existed during the early sixties expand in order to take care of the increased demand seemed an invitation to disaster. Much of what was available was provided by relatively untrained personnel in less than desirable physical settings. Standards of quality and regulatory procedures in most states were minimal.

This fear of the negative consequences of child care also pervaded the minds of the general public, including child-care clients. Parents felt guilty about utilizing the very service that was to provide "care and protection" for their children. To some extent this fear was due to the incredibly bad press received by child care.[13] Writers and commentators often seemed to be on search-and-destroy missions where child care was concerned. Any malfeasance suspected or discovered (sexual abuse being the most outstanding example) received front-page and evening-news coverage, whereas the developmental support provided in quality care was never newsworthy. Child care, neglected and ignored by policymakers for decades, was suddenly a big political issue—and a destructive one. Conservative politicians and the citizens' groups that backed them began to accuse child care in the abstract for all the ills of modern life. Adjectives applied to the service were consistently pejorative and negative. Some of these are highlighted in Table 1. Certainly the most damaging from the standpoint were the charges that child care was "family-weakening" and that it somehow represented a communal approach to child-rearing.

Although the field has not totally recovered from these charges, they have less impact in today's world. Again, help has come from the inexorable march of demographics. When a social custom (such as the utilization of child care) becomes the modal pattern for a culture — that is, when the proportion of the population using it crosses the 50 percent line — that custom begins to take on a new meaning within the culture. Within the past decade, this cultural shift has definitely occurred with respect to public attitudes toward child care in America.

MISTRUST OF EDUCATION

At present, the strongest mistrust appears to be of education; for the first time in its modern history, child care is basking in the glow of public support. Some of the mistrust is of the hysterical, overgeneralizing type: "The schools have already ruined our big kids. Let's not turn the little ones over to them and let them do the same thing to them." Others fear the consequences of subjecting young children to the legal battles and the high-frequency change of setting and personnel that have characterized public education for several decades.

Much of the fear appears to stem from what is perceived, legitimately or otherwise, as an excessive emphasis on academic learning at the expense of developmentally appropriate activities in any setting that is considered primarily "education" without much concern for "care." If the education–child care linkage is vertical as well as horizontal, as it was at Kramer, there is a particularly strong fear that a downward push of the curriculum is inevitable. That is, what is now first grade will be taught during the kindergarten year, the kindergarten will be pushed down to four-year-olds, and so on. Many persons who are strong advocates for *both* child care and education, such as Ed Zigler,[14] have voiced this concern.

In expressions of concern on this score, a key term is often "formal education." By this term is generally meant heavy reliance on seated teaching exercises with dittoed sheets and workbooks rather than informal, hands-on, free-choice learning activities. Although there are no data to support the claim, the assumption is made that such activities occur more frequently in educationally oriented early childhood programs than they do in those more child-care oriented.

One vitally concerned group that offers few if any objections to a move toward truly integrated services is the corps of professionals and paraprofessionals who staff early childhood programs. This is perhaps paradoxical, as teachers and caregivers are so typically underpaid and overworked that they have a right to feel hostile toward both banners. We tend to think of both education and child care as somehow publicly funded services. To be sure, sometimes they are, but there are still thousands of certified teachers working in small private kindergartens and child-care centers who receive only about two-thirds of the salary that similarly trained teachers would receive in a public school or child-care center. Some minimally trained child caregivers worry that total educational auspices for early childhood services will deprive them of employment opportunities. For the most part, however, they welcome this endorsement of the fact that they have indeed been providing education all along. In spite of low salaries and long hours, the biggest complaint of many child caregivers is that the importance of their work is not appreciated. Many think that more complete integration of child care and education will remedy this problem.

DEVELOPMENTS AT THE FRONTIER

At the time of this writing, the field of early childhood services is expanding rapidly. Educational reform—in the air all over the nation—rarely neglects the importance of the early years for helping children start their educational careers on a solid foundation. Corporations are paying more attention to child care and are beginning to vie with one another in the development of programs that will support families and children. Several major national bills offering support for both personnel training and operating costs are in the works and have a good likelihood of being passed into law. Both major political parties, instead of denouncing child care or avoiding any mention of it in a platform in fear of losing votes, are now calling for increased funding and various measures that will improve quality.

In all these activities, there appears to be a conceptual advance over the position assumed a decade ago—that is, there is now a recognition that high-quality early childhood programs must be comprehensive, integrated programs. This represents a quantum leap upward and forward for the field. The big challenge now for professionals and advocates who shape the directions of future growth is to make certain that we do not allow our own provincialism and partisan histories to foster a return to compartmentalization and divisiveness where there should be unity and collaboration.

Notes

1   Child Welfare League of America, *Standards for Day Care Service* (New York: Child Welfare League of America, 1960), p. 2.

2   George S. Morrison, "Maria Montessori," in his *Early Childhood Education Today* (Columbus, Ohio: Charles E. Merrill, 1976), pp. 33–57.

3   Robert R. Rusk, "Robert Owen," in his *A History of Infant Education* (London: University of London Press Ltd., 1967), pp. 119–34.

4   Margaret McMillan, *The Nursery School* (London: J. M. Dent & Sons, 1919).

5   I have personally written more than twenty-nine articles, beginning as early as 1967

and continuing to the present, urging recognition of the reality that early childhood education and child care represent one unified service model that may vary quantitatively. See, for example, Bettye M. Caldwell and Julius B. Richmond, "The Children's Center—A Microcosmic Health, Education, and Welfare Unit," in *Early Child Care: The New Perspectives*, ed. L. Dittman (New York: Atherton Press, 1968), pp. 326–58, 373–77; and Bettye M. Caldwell, "Day Care and Early Environmental Adequacy," in *Early Experience and the Development of Competence*, ed. William Fowler (San Francisco: Jossey Bass, 1986), pp. 11–30. I have also given at least one hundred major addresses dealing in some way with this subject. Such efforts have in the main represented the well-known phenomenon of preaching to the choir, in that the readers and listeners were largely practitioners in the field who, in their daily lives, lived integrated services and did not need to be persuaded to their authenticity.

6   U.S. Bureau of the Census, *Women in the American Economy*, Current Population Reports, Special Studies Series P-23, No. 146 (Washington, D.C.: U.S. Department of Commerce, 1987), p. 7.

7   Ibid.

8   Phyllis T. Elardo and Bettye M. Caldwell, "The Kramer Adventure: A School for the Future," in *Childhood Education* 50 (January 1974): 143–52. Most of the major components of the Kramer Project are still in operation, albeit in a different school and minus the research support. The complete merger of the child-care and education components of the project remain intact, however.

9   Although we consistently referred to Kramer as an extended-day school, trying to emphasize the fact that the extra hours and days were educational as well as protective, the name never caught hold. No matter how hard we tried to eliminate any distinction between the educational and child-care services, the language used by staff, parents, and children revealed that the semantic set, that the two were separate services, was difficult to break. At the end of the "regular" school day, most children would say, as they reported to the check-in point for the extended-day activities, "I'm going down to day care now." That kind of verbal habit is difficult to break.

10   Some of these older children were like unpaid employees of the project. They loved to "help" with the younger children—especially the babies—and to share the companionship possible with the early childhood teachers that was not considered appropriate with their elementary teachers.

11   Kramer was the oldest school in Little Rock, with the original part having been constructed in 1895. A new and much larger school was being built with a beautifully designed early childhood wing instead of the adapted or portable classrooms housing the early childhood program at Kramer. However, the emotional attachment to Kramer was so strong that even the promise of a new building did not mitigate the pain associated with its loss.

12   Dorothy Hewes and Barbara Hartman, *Early Childhood Education: A Workbook for Administrators* (San Francisco: R and E Research Associates, 1972), pp. 21–22.

13   Bettye M. Caldwell, "How Can We Educate the American Public about the Child Care Profession," *Young Children* 38 (1983): 11–17.

14   Edward Zigler, "Formal School for Four-year-olds? No," in *Early Schooling The National Debate*, ed. S. L. Kagan and E. F. Zigler (New Haven: Yale University Press, 1987), pp. 27–44.

An Early Childhood Center Developmental Model for Public School Settings

GUY P. HASKINS, SAMUEL J. ALESSI, JR.
Buffalo Public Schools, New York

When the federal court ordered Buffalo to desegregate, the school system took its mandate to be a curriculum and instruction challenge of the highest order. The result, Buffalo's highly successful Early Childhood Centers, is described and evaluated in this article in terms of student achievement, parental involvement, and racial balancing.

On April 30, 1976, Judge John T. Curtin of the Federal District Court ordered the Buffalo Public School system to desegregate. His judgment found that the city schools were illegally imbalanced with respect to racial composition, and that it was incumbent on the district to devise a plan that would address this problem while simultaneously providing viable educational programs.

The Buffalo City School Board responded by beginning implementation of a plan for gradual desegregation. Phase I in 1976 and Phase II in 1977 included closing some schools and creating several new magnet centers. Then, on June 19, 1980, Phase III of the school board's plan was approved. It established six Early Childhood Centers, with student assignments made on a voluntary basis. Phase IIIx was approved on May 19, 1981. That part of the plan mandated a pre-kindergarten through second grade format for the six original schools, and it created four new Early Childhood Centers with fixed assignments.

This article describes the development and implementation of Buffalo's Early Childhood Centers, and their evaluation with respect to student achievement and parental attitudes. It also examines Buffalo's early childhood center design as a tool for desegregation and school improvement.

As large city school systems become increasingly multicultural, and as schools, in general, become involved in early childhood education, models are needed that are responsive both to the needs of young children and their families and to society's demands for effective schools. Buffalo's Early Childhood Center Program meets these criteria and can serve as a model to other school systems seeking to integrate quality early education into their existing school structures.

BACKGROUND

Buffalo, the second largest city in New York State, covers an area of approximately 43 square miles. Its population is just under 400,000. Buffalo has experienced a growth pattern similar to that of other large industrial cities of the Northeast: The population expanded within fixed city boundaries until 1950 and then steadily declined with suburban migration and the loss of regional industries. By the early 1970s, there had been a major decline in the school population with a disproportionate decrease in the majority-to-minority ratio and a concomitant increase in the number of students from families at lower economic and educational levels.

The majority of Buffalo residents are English speaking; however, there are significant numbers of Hispanic, Italian, and Asian groups who speak little or no English. The city is settled in neighborhoods with strong ethnic concentrations and boundaries that can be readily defined. Neighborhood patterns have remained relatively stable over the years due to both geographic characteristics and transportation routes, which make certain areas of the city less accessible than others. This neighborhood settlement pattern has had a direct and definite impact on the Buffalo Public Schools, complicating the district's efforts to achieve racial balance throughout the system.

Within this setting, Buffalo, a fiscally dependent district, is responsible for the education of approximately 47,000 students at seventy-nine school sites. This makes Buffalo, in terms of students, the largest single school district in New York State outside of New York City. The current student enrollment ratio is approximately 45 percent majority to 55 percent minority. Of that minority enrollment, approximately 47 percent are black, 5 percent are Hispanic, 2 percent are Native American, and 1 percent are Asian. Operating within the district, there are approximately fifty-seven nonpublic schools with a total enrollment of just over 14,000 students.

Services provided by the district are comprehensive. They include early childhood, elementary, magnet, academic secondary, technical and vocational, special education, bilingual, gifted/talented, and alternative programs. Since 1974, the Buffalo school district has been governed by an elected school board composed of nine individuals, six representing specific voting districts within the city and three serving as at-large members.

THE EARLY CHILDHOOD CENTER (ECC) PROGRAM

The program design is best understood in the context of the history of the project. The design, in turn, has helped determine some of the current directions of the project, leading to realization of the broad, original aims of the effort. Each of those dimensions is summarized briefly below.

HISTORY

The decision to implement the six original Early Childhood Center programs as part of the city's desegregation plan was shaped by two factors: the need at the elementary school level for improved compliance with the 1976 court order, and increasing evidence of the substantive long-term benefits of quality early childhood education.[1]

A year before the Early Childhood Centers were established, Buffalo's associate superintendent for instructional services called together a group of early childhood specialists from within the public schools to begin planning. This committee studied the data on students currently attending the identified sites for the centers and on the prospective students from designated feeder schools. The initial structure of the program at the centers was designed, and the goals of the centers were prepared. The committee then reorganized and expanded into the Early Childhood Steering Committee. Included in this committee were the original specialists in early childhood education, elementary principals, supervisors of elementary education, support staff, teachers, and parents. The steering committee was charged with the responsibility for developing a full program designed to meet the specific needs of the children scheduled to attend the centers.

During the organizational year, 1980–1981, six buildings were chosen for centers because of their inner-city locations and high minority enrollment. Each of these centers was paired with "feeder" schools chosen for their high majority populations and accessibility to the designated Early Childhood Centers. Five of the schools that had included grades K–8 retained their grades 3–8 population for that first year. In September 1981, to satisfy community requests and further desegregate the school system, four additional Early Childhood Centers were established. This was Phase IIIx of the desegregation plan, and it brought to ten the number of ECCs in the Buffalo program. In that same 1981–1982 school year, all the 3–8 classes were transferred from the original ECCs to their paired feeder schools. Finally, two of the new ECCs became all-city centers and accepted applicants from additional areas of the Buffalo district.

The centers were established in inner-city schools to promote integration. By establishing an improved academic program and eliminating grades 3–8, the Early Childhood schools, it was anticipated, would act as magnets to draw majority children into the inner city. The 3–8 grades were to be bused to peripheral schools. Feeder patterns were designed to provide a sense of community: Children would be able to establish friendships lasting throughout their school years.

Student selection for the Early Childhood Centers was accomplished through a lottery since there were more applicants than there were spaces for them. The lottery system assured that there were equal numbers of minority and majority children and boys and girls in each class. Children in grades K–2 were assigned to their district's Early Childhood Center; then, for integration purposes, students were assigned from the feeder schools in order to balance the classes racially.

PROGRAM DESIGN

The Early Childhood Center program was designed

to facilitate improved levels of student performance in both reading and mathematics;

to assist in the development of positive parental attitudes and perceptions relative to the child care, socialization, and academic components of the ECC program; and

to facilitate the desegregation of each Early Childhood Center to within the 30 to 65 percent minority composition guidelines established by the court ruling.

To work toward these goals, and following discussions and evaluations with consultants from the National Diffusion Network, the steering committee chose three programs that had been nationally validated by the U.S. Department of Education. These were to be replicated at the Early Childhood Centers. Buffalo's adoption of the three models marked the first time that these programs were combined at a single school and coordinated into a comprehensive effort to address the needs of young children.

1. The *Early Intervention Program* was adapted from *Early Prevention of School Failure (EPSF)*, originally validated in Peotone, Illinois. Upon entering the Early Childhood Centers at the kindergarten or pre-kindergarten level, each child is screened to determine needs, strengths, and learning modes or styles. Children are screened in the following modality areas: Gross Motor, Fine Motor, Auditory Skills, Visual Skills, and Language Skills. Among instruments used are the PLS — Preschool Language Scale, the MAS — Motor Activity Scale, the VMI — Visual Motor Integration, the PPVT — Peabody Picture Vocabulary Test, and the DAM — Draw-a-Man Test. The results of the screening are reviewed, parent observation forms are compiled, children are grouped according to needs and strengths, and a sequential basic skill development program is planned for each child.

2. The *Talents Unlimited Program (TU)* was originally validated in Mobile, Alabama. A planned program to develop thinking abilities is important to success in the working world as well as in school. These talents include pro-

ductive thinking, communication, planning, forecasting, and decision making. However, TU is not approached in isolation. Instead, students are given increased opportunities to develop in reading, mathematics, and science, and to acquire knowledge through using many different ways of thinking.

3. *Systematic Teaching and Measuring Mathematics (STAMM)* is a comprehensive, sequential, manipulative mathematics program through which each child's performance is carefully observed and recorded. It provides for continuous progress through the mathematics curriculum. Classrooms contain various concrete mathematics materials that aid the child with an experiential approach. STAMM was originally validated in Jefferson County, Colorado.

In addition to the programs cited, Buffalo's ECC model incorporates a grade-level structure of all-day pre-kindergarten, all-day kindergarten, grade one, and grade two. The framework of full-day kindergarten and full-day pre-kindergarten was intended to increase contact time with pupils, the anticipated result being enhanced student performance in both reading and mathematics. Also, the length of the school day was attractive to working parents who had a need for child care. In order to address continuity of instruction in a highly mobile system, each ECC program teacher was familiarized with the curriculum for all grade levels. This approach was specifically intended to strengthen parent confidence in the overall program and to encourage willingness to participate in the desegregation program.

Every classroom of the Early Childhood Centers was designed to include a teacher and a teacher aide. Each center was also to have a curriculum coordinator, who would provide training and ongoing instructional assistance. In fact, the ECC program provided for extensive staff development. In order to be accepted initially, professional staff who applied for positions had to pass two interviews and make a commitment to attend regular in-service training sessions. In succeeding years, only one interview was required.

Strong efforts were made to effect a close alliance between home and school by involving parents in all phases of their children's activities in the Early Childhood Centers. Parents were asked to complete observation forms during the initial screening process. This occasioned a sharing experience: The parents provided information on the child's growth and development while the teacher described the school's educational program. Additional opportunities for keeping parents as programmatic partners have been and continue to be significant aspects of the overall design.[2]

CURRENT PROGRAM

The current program is both conceptually and practically in keeping with the original design. It now includes eleven centers serving pre-kindergarten to second grade and involves approximately 5,800 students in over two hundred classrooms. The full-day program is being maintained for all four grades (pre-kindergarten, kindergarten, one, and two). Staffing continues with a full-time teacher and a full-time teacher aide in each classroom.

At the school district level, a full-time administrator coordinates the program and a supervisor evaluates teacher performance. In addition to this staff, a reading teacher and a math teacher visit all centers to keep the program cohesive. They are able to present new ideas and assist teachers in planning effective instruction.

At the school level, each principal has a full-time coordinator who is responsible for training new personnel and facilitating the screening and testing of students. The three special programs—Talents, Early Intervention, and STAMM—are combined with the general early childhood curriculum in all areas, including reading, mathematics, language arts, social studies, science, and outdoor play. Principals and coordinators meet with the director once a month for communication, coordination of efforts, sharing of information, and planning future activities. Constant evaluation of the instructional program (including reinforcement activities, flexibility of grouping, and sequential skills development) and constant monitoring of parental involvement take place in the schools. Results are compiled by evaluators in the central office.

Originally, staff training took place in the summer. At that time, the three National Diffusion Network programs were presented by local turnkey trainers. Now, in the eighth year of the program, the training of new teachers takes place by using five substitute days during the school year. Teacher aides are trained by the coordinators in each building. Staff development includes training in all early childhood instructional program content, diagnostic techniques, and intervention and prevention strategies. The major concern is to provide a rich academic, social, and emotional environment within which optimum educational growth will be possible.

EVALUATION

Program evaluation has been ongoing since the inception of the Early Childhood Center model in the 1980–1981 school year. Using a systems-analytic approach, the evaluation has focused on outcomes of the three major program goals: Student achievement; development of positive parental attitudes and increased parental participation and commitment; and facilitating desegregation within the district.

STUDENT ACHIEVEMENT (PROGRAM GOAL 1)

Hypothesis: Through the implementation of diagnostic/prescriptive instructional programs such as EPSF, TU, and STAMM, the academic performance levels of grade 1 and grade 2 participants will demonstrate positive and statistically significant differences in both reading and mathematics when compared with total district results.

Sample Selection The schools selected to document this component of our ECC program are the ten facilities that were operational as part of Phase III and Phase IIIx of the Buffalo Desegregation Plan. The control schools are the remaining elementary schools in the district.

Assessment Techniques Program assessment instrumentation represents appropriate forms and levels of the Metropolitan Achievement Test (78), the Stanford Achievement Test (82), and the California Test of Basic Skills (82). Table 1 identifies this instrumentation by subject matter area, grade level, and program year.

Table 1. Reading/Math Instrumentation

Grade	School Years	Test*	Reading Form	Level	Mathematics Test*	Form	Level
1	1980–1984	MAT (78)	TS	Primary 1	MAT (78)	TS	Primary 1
	1985–1987	CTBS (82)	U	C	SAT (82)	F	Primary 1
2	1980–1984	MAT (78)	TS	Primary 2	MAT (78)	TS	Primary 2
	1985-1987	CTBS (82)	U	C	SAT (82)	F	Primary 2

*MAT — Metropolitan Achievement Test (1978); CTBS — California Test of Basic Skills (1982); SAT — Stanford Achievement Test (1982).

All student testing data were obtained from spring administrations of our City-Wide Achievement Testing Program, conducted in the first two weeks of May for each school year. National norms with a standardization midpoint of April 20 were utilized for interpretive purposes. Consequently, the district testing dates fall well within the standardization window set for the Metropolitan Achievement Test (MAT), the California Test of Basic Skills (CTBS), and the Stanford Achievement Test (SAT).

Validity The appropriateness (validity) of the testing instrumentation for the target group was determined on the basis of two primary criteria. The first factor was the finding by the Buffalo Public Schools' Test Selection Committee that test content was consistent with state and district curricula in reading and mathematics. The second factor was the extent to which questions concerning the content, construct, and predictive validity of the MAT (78) were addressed by the Psychological Corporation in development and construction of the test series. These two considerations were thoroughly discussed and were the main determinants in the decision to utilize the MAT (78) in the district's City-Wide Achievement Testing Program. These concerns were also the primary factors considered in changing to the CTBS (82) in mathematics for the 1984–1985 school year.

Evaluation Design It was recognized that a classical experimental design incorporating the matching of schools on relevant variables and then random assignment to either the ECC Program or to a comparison group school was not possible. Consequently, a quasi-experimental design featuring a comparison between ECC schools and the remaining schools in the district for each of the spring 1980–1981 through 1986–1987 data collection points was utilized.

It is important to note that the potential for systematic bias with respect to ECC student enrollment was addressed through a lottery procedure at the pre-K level and by the feeder pattern in assigning students in grades K through 2. The expressed intent of this procedure was not only to ensure racial balance, but also to prevent "brain drain" from the remaining schools in the district. This strategy was indeed successful in that mathematics and reading comparison results do not systematically favor the ECC schools until the implementation (third) year of the program has been completed. For both the organizational and developmental years, systematic differences in performance levels were not observed between ECC and control schools.

Data Presentation/Statistical Comparison   A chi square (X^2) data-analytic procedure was used to examine differences in levels of student performance in mathematics and reading. The data for both ECC and control group schools are distributed as the number/percentage of students falling into stanines 1–3, 4–6, and 7–9. The chi square procedure was conducted in order to determine if the stanine distributions for each group are independent of one another across year, grade, and subject matter categories.

Educational Significance   Tables 2–5 provide strong evidence to support program impact with respect to the academic (M/R) achievement of ECC students. These observations take on even greater import when it is considered that the control group schools contain all of the remaining first- and second-grade students in the district.

Table 2.   Grade 1 Comparisons in Reading (Early Childhood Centers/Control Group)

| School | Group | Stanine Distribution | | | Total | X^2 | Sig. |
		Low % 1–3	Med. % 4–6	High % 7–9	(N)		
1980–1981	ECC*	24	64	12	(508)	19.4	.01
	Control	32	53	14	(3,365)		
1981–1982†	ECC	32	58	10	(894)	3.3	NS
	Control	30	58	12	(2,645)		
1982–1983	ECC*	23	61	16	(1,129)	25.7	.01
	Control	31	56	13	(2,325)		
1983–1984	ECC*	20	58	22	(1,373)	6.1	.05
	Control	22	59	19	(2,341)		

Table 2. Grade 1 Comparisons in Reading (Early Childhood Centers/Control Group) (Continued)

School	Group	Stanine Distribution			Total (N)	X^2	Sig.
		Low %1-3	Med. %4-6	High %7-9			
1984–1985	ECC*	21	61	18	(1,339)	14.8	.01
	Control	27	58	15	(1,999)		
1985–1986	ECC*	20	59	21	(1,424)	40.3	.01
	Control	28	57	15	(1,979)		
1986–1987	ECC*	15	60	25	(1,506)	44.4	.01
	Control	22	60	18	(2,045)		

*Dominant group.
†New schools become operational at this point, so time series results reflect a mix of first and second year programs.

Table 3. Grade 1 Comparisons in Mathematics (Early Childhood Centers/Control Group)

School	Group	Stanine Distribution			Total (N)	X^2	Sig.
		Low %1-3	Med. %4-6	High %7-9			
1980–1981	ECC*	22	52	26	(506)	10.3	.01
	Control	26	54	20	(3,365)		
1981–1982†	ECC	43	45	12	(892)	109.7	.01
	Control*	21	56	23	(2,656)		
1982–1983	ECC*	17	56	27	(1,128)	35.6	.01
	Control	26	51	23	(2,332)		
1983–1984	ECC*	15	51	34	(1,371)	28.4	.01
	Control	20	53	27	(2,332)		
1984–1985	ECC*	16	53	31	(1,347)	43.4	.01
	Control	24	53	23	(2,009)		
1985–1986	ECC*	14	52	34	(1,395)	72.0	.01
	Control	25	52	23	(1,980)		
1986–1987	ECC*	12	52	36	(1,495)	78.5	.01
	Control	21	55	24	(2,037)		

*Dominant group.
†New schools become operational at this point, so time series results reflect a mix of first and second year programs.

Table 4.   Grade 2 Comparisons in Reading (Early Childhood Centers/ Control Group)

| School | Group | Stanine Distribution | | | Total | X^2 | Sig. |
		Low %1–3	Med. %4–6	High %7–9	(N)		
1980–1981	ECC	40	52	8	(463)	26.8	.01
	Control*	29	58	13	(3,181)		
1981–1982†	ECC	34	58	8	(738)	14.3	.01
	Control*	33	54	13	(2,533)		
1982–1983	ECC*	28	59	13	(1,118)	8.7	.05
	Control	33	55	12	(2,145)		
1983–1984	ECC*	21	59	20	(1,158)	8.8	.05
	Control	25	59	16	(2,051)		
1984–1985	ECC*	24	48	28	(1,163)	29.0	.01
	Control	31	48	21	(2,029)		
1985–1986	ECC*	18	53	29	(1,289)	40.5	.01
	Control	28	48	24	(1,882)		
1986–1987	ECC*	17	52	31	(1,211)	15.9	.01
	Control	23	50	27	(1,907)		

*Dominant group.
†New schools become operational at this point, so time series results reflect a mix of first and second year programs.

Table 5.   Grade 2 Comparisons in Mathematics (Early Childhood Centers/Control Group)

| School | Group | Stanine Distribution | | | Total | X^2 | Sig. |
		Low %1–3	Med. %4–6	High %7–9	(N)		
1980–1981	ECC	21	57	22	(461)	1.33	NS
	Control	19	59	22	(3,170)		
1981–1982†	ECC	22	59	19	(736)	.1214	NS
	Control	22	58	20	(2,533)		
1982–1983	ECC*	19	57	24	(1,119)	15.9	.01
	Control	24	56	20	(2,141)		
1983–1984	ECC*	11	53	36	(1,151)	41.3	.01
	Control	17	56	27	(2,069)		

Table 5.   Grade 2 Comparisons in Mathematics (Early Childhood Centers/Control Group) (Continued)

School	Group	Stanine Distribution			Total (N)	X^2	Sig.
		Low %1-3	Med. %4-6	High %7-9			
1984–1985	ECC*	15	46	39	(1,162)	59.2	.01
	Control	23	50	27	(2,033)		
1985–1986	ECC*	11	50	39	(1,282)	31.7	.01
	Control	18	51	31	(1,883)		
1986–1987	ECC*	9	48	43	(1,287)	28.9	.01
	Control	4	52	34	(1,893)		

*Dominant group.
†New schools become operational at this point, so time series results reflect a mix of first and second year programs.

Given the random (lottery) assignment of students to the ECC program, the data pattern that emerges from the comparisons conducted documents the following:

1. That during the first two years of program implementation (organization–development) control-group students are likely to perform as well or better than ECC students in mathematics and/or reading.
2. That beginning in the third (implementation) program year, the ECC students systematically perform at a statistically significant and higher level in both reading and mathematics than do the control-group comparisons.

Consequently, in terms of a systems developmental approach, it should be noted that performance level differences favoring program participants may or may not occur prior to the third year of program operation. However, once the third year has been completed, program outcomes systematically favor the ECC students. This finding strongly suggests that at this point both operational and programmatic components of the program are functioning at the same level and are having an impact on student-performance outcomes in a very positive manner. It is the combination of performance-level outcomes and systems developmental actualization that makes a cogent argument for "a program at the end of the bus ride" approach to voluntary desegregation.

PARENTAL ATTITUDES/PERCEPTIONS (PROGRAM GOAL 2)

Goal: To assess parental perceptions and attitudes toward the learning experiences and activities of their children in terms of the total child care, socialization, and academic components of the Early Childhood Center Program.

Sample Selection   The schools selected to document this component of the ECC program again represent the ten facilities that were operationalized as part of Phase III and Phase IIIx of the Buffalo Integration/Desegregation Plan. Data were obtained for pre-kindergarten, kindergarten, grade 1, and grade 2 parent groups at each facility, with approximately twenty Early Childhood Center Parent Surveys distributed at each grade level. A 30 percent randomly selected sample was then identified for program evaluative purposes.

Assessment Techniques   The Early Childhood Center Parent Survey consists of fourteen items representing total child care, socialization, and academic program factors. In addition, there was a section provided for further comment or clarification of ratings. Figure 1 presents a breakdown of survey items by program factor/components.

Validity and Reliability   The content validity of statements contained in the Early Childhood Center Parent Survey was determined by the director of the Early Childhood Center programs, two center teachers, a district supervisor of evaluation, and the director of the SUNY/Buffalo Early Childhood Research Center.

The procedure for identifying, classifying, and presenting statements contained in the survey is outlined below:

1. Agreement within the group about what the key program factors/ components of the ECC program were (e.g., total child care, socialization, academic).

2. Examination and modification of a large number of statements concerning early childhood programs, education, socialization factors, and so forth, in order to ensure that they were appropriate operational descriptors of the ECC program.

3. Placement of these statements into the three program factor/component categories identified. This placement required at least 75 percent consensus of opinion within the committee.

4. Selection of an appropriate rating scale and choice points: 1 = Strongly Disagree; 2 = Disagree; 3 = Uncertain; 4 = Agree; 5 = Strongly Agree.

5. Development of appropriate directions and respondent information.

The reliability of the ECC Parent Survey cannot be demonstrated by use of either a test administration/readministration paradigm or a split half/ KR_{20} estimate of internal consistency approach. Consequently, an examination of the reliability of the ECC Parent Survey was considered to be noncritical with respect to this aspect of our evaluation.

Evaluation Design   The formal evaluation of parental involvement features

Program Factor/ Component	Item No.	
Total Child Care	1	One of the important features of the Early Childhood Centers is the extended day for pre-kindergarten and kindergarten.
	2	Parent involvement and participation in the Early Childhood Center Program is important.
	3	Another important aspect of the Early Childhood Center program is the development of positive attitudes toward school.
	4	The Early Childhood Center Program puts a strong emphasis on the development of good behavior in the children.
Socialization	5	One part of the Early Childhood Center Program should and does focus on providing experiences in which all children learn how to work, play, and compete with each other.
	6	In the Early Childhood Center Program there should be no activities solely for boys or solely for girls.
	7	Other children in the family can learn from a brother or sister who attends an Early Childhood Center.
	8	The Early Childhood Centers provide an opportunity for both parents and children from different cultural and ethnic backgrounds to better appreciate and understand one another.
	9	A major program emphasis of the Early Childhood Center is to develop good learning habits in the children.
	10	The Early Childhood Center focus is on helping the child.
	11	One of the services the Early Childhood Centers provide is special programming to help meet the child's needs and deal with each child's problems.
Academic	12	The Early Childhood Center program emphasizes the development of vocabulary, math, and language skills in children.
	13	Because of participation in the Early Childhood Center Program, it is quite likely that a child will achieve more rapidly in later grades.
	14	The Early Childhood Center provides adequate exploratory experiences and special activities in the form of in-class and out-of-class activities.

Figure 1. Early Childhood Center Parent Survey (Breakdown of Items by Program Factors/Components)

a comparison of the ECC Parent Survey Rating Scale Distributions for the 1981–1982 school year, the development year, and the 1983–1984 and 1986–1987 operational years of the program. In this comparison, the 1981–1982 data serve as a baseline for the 1983–1984 and 1986–1987 comparisons.

Data Presentation/Statistical Comparison Table 6 presents parent response data for the "agree" and "strongly agree" categories of the five-point Parent Survey Rating Scale. These results document parent response distributions that are positive across each of the program factors examined. This outcome is indicative of a very desirable level of parental awareness and is useful in determining programmatic effects at different stages of systems development.

Table 6.   ECC Parent Survey Data

Program Factor/ Components	% Agree/Strongly Agree Responses by Data Collection Point		
	Point #1 (1981–1982)	Point #2 (1983–1984)	Point #3 (1986–1987)
Child Care	89	94	84*
Socialization	85	90	90
Academic	92	94	93

*This regression may be more a function of the need to redefine the term "extended day" in item one of the ECC Parent Survey than an indicator of change in parental perceptions with respect to the child care component of the ECC program. For example, at data collection point 1 (1981–1982), the term was clearly understood to represent the distinction between full-day pre-K and kindergarten instruction and one-half day service. At data point 3, the term includes an additional connotation of hours either prior to or following the school day, hours that are not part of the ECC program.

Educational Significance   For each of the three program factors assessed by the parent survey, patterns of parental response are very favorable. These findings indicate that:

1. With the exception of the regression noted and a drop of one percentage point on perception of the academic component for 1986–1987, increasingly more positive perceptions of ECC program effectiveness are being recorded at each data collection point.
2. There is a high degree of consensus that parental involvement is an important part of the total ECC program.
3. Opportunities for social development and awareness are very positively perceived features of the program.
4. The educational function performed by the ECC is perceived as meeting both basic and curricular needs in addition to providing adequate exploratory experiences for the students.
5. Current student performance is perceived as being enhanced and future learning potential as being facilitated by ECC participation.

DESEGREGATION (PROGRAM GOAL 3)

Goal: To facilitate the desegregation of each Early Childhood Center to within the 30–65 percent minority guidelines established by the U.S. District Court ruling of 1976.

Sample Selection   The schools selected to document this component represent the ten facilities that were operational as part of Phases III and IIIx of the Buffalo Integration/Desegregation Plan.

Assessment Techniques   Racial/ethnic data is collected in October of every school year. This information is published as the ethnic census of the Buffalo Public Schools by the Division of Finance, Research, and Personnel of the Buffalo Board of Education.

Validity and Reliability   The validity and reliability of the ethnic census data are subject to reporting and informational guidelines established by the Department of Finance, Research, and Personnel.

Evaluation Design   The evaluation design for this program component features a comparison of majority/minority ratios with the 30–65 percent criterion level established by the federal court mandate. This comparison has been examined for the organizational and development years, 1980–1981 and 1981–1982, and for each successive implementation year up to and including the 1986–1987 counts. The 1978–1979 school year serves as a baseline.

Data Presentation/Statistical Comparison   Table 7 presents ethnic census data with respect to minority group composition for ECCs across organizational, developmental, implementational, and operational years. These data indicate a steady increase of majority students within the ECC schools. In addition, beginning with the 1981–1982 developmental year, ECC majority/minority ratios had fallen within the limits established by the 1976 court ruling.

Table 7.   ECC Minority Group Comparison Data

School Year	1978–1979	1980–1981*	1981–1982†	1982–1983	1983–1984	1984–1985	1985–1986	1986–1987
Percent minority	85.8	69.8	61.8	63.3	63.0	62.8	60.6	61.2
Percent majority	14.2	30.2	38.2	36.8	37.0	37.2	39.4	38.8

*ECC Program organizational year.
†Developmental year; four new schools became operational at this time.

Educational Significance   ECC ethnic distribution data are interesting in two very specific ways. First, they indicate a willingness on the part of majority parents to send their children to schools in the inner city that previously had a predominantly minority enrollment. Second, when taken into consideration with parent participation and attitudinal data, they are an index of both parental awareness of what the ECC program is all about and of their satisfaction with its effectiveness and operation.

It is from within this context that the ECC program as a quality educational vehicle to promote integration/desegregation within the Buffalo Public Schools has been an absolute and unqualified success — not only in terms of racial balance, but also in terms of academic excellence and parental involvement.

INFORMAL PROGRAM EFFECTIVENESS INFORMATION

The comments, observations, and activities listed here are program descriptors emerging from the total project activity that cut across the academic-achievement, parental-involvement, and racial-balance goals of the ECC program. These statements represent only a fraction of the information that has been collected and maintained in order to document effective ECC operation.

1. The Early Childhood Centers were selected in 1984 to implement a pilot program to aid young children with sickle cell disease. This program was cooperatively developed by the Buffalo Public Schools, the Buffalo Children's Hospital, and the Sickle Cell Association of Western New York.

2. Each year a program survey is conducted to assess parent views of the ECC program. Each year, at least 90 percent of the parents surveyed were positive in their assessment of the program. This outcome is even more significant when it is realized that the percentage of parents who completed the survey represents 78 percent of those asked to respond.

3. As an example of national recognition of the ECC program, consider that a teacher from Kobuk, Alaska, asked the Early Prevention of School Failure office in Peotone, Illinois, about the best early childhood program in the country. It was suggested that she visit Buffalo's ECC program.

4. For the first time, an EPSF Leadership Certification Seminar and Training Program was held outside of Illinois when it was held at Buffalo's ECC 78 in April 1983. An early childhood conference on April 29, 1983, culminated the five-day program. It was sponsored by the Buffalo Public Schools in cooperation with the New York State Education Department Office of Federal Demonstration Programs and with EPSF. The seminar drew participants from throughout the country.

5. Student retention rates at grade level for ECCs are 3 to 4 percent lower than district retention rates for the same grades.

6. About forty Region II Head Start directors and teachers from New York, New Jersey, and Puerto Rico visited Buffalo's ECCs in October 1985 as part of the annual Early Childhood Conference program.

7. Numerous visitors from throughout the United States, as well as from countries such as Australia, the Sudan, Japan, and Jamaica, have observed the ECCs in order to view an exemplary program and to examine integration/desegregation methods utilized in large urban districts.

CONCLUSION

What the authors have described so far is the development, implementation, and evaluation of Buffalo's Early Childhood Center program. It is most important, however, to put this entire description into an overall context: curriculum planning. Even though the immediate impetus for this program was a federal court order dealing with the "negative" issue of segregation, the Buffalo Public Schools viewed it as a positive opportunity for educational improvement. This was only normal since we generally refuse to look at any changes in district operation without considering implications and/or possibilities that such changes have for improving a student's education. In other words, *any* organizational, operational, and/or programmatic change is considered in terms of good curriculum planning.

An order to desegregate thus became an opportunity to redesign program and meant that we had to consider goals and teaching/learning strategies. In so doing, the instructional concerns we addressed for ECCs were the same as we address for any other level of education — elementary, middle, or secondary — and the collaborative and cooperative involvement that we maintained was the same as we attempt to maintain for any level of education. This means explicitly seeking the input and considering the issues raised by parents, students, teachers, administrators, and board of education members. It means addressing costs and activities, learning theory and the experience of practice, research results and possible replications. It also means careful attention to vertical articulation: How can the curriculum and instructional program of the ECC inform and lead positively toward the curriculum and instructional program of the elementary school?

In Buffalo, these were some of our concerns and questions. We believe our procedures and our answers have been such as to assure positive academic and social gains, and to assure movement toward attainment of our goals. Our beliefs have also had a fair measure of outside confirmation since the Buffalo Public Schools have received more state and federal awards for schools of excellence than any other district in the nation. Two of the thirteen schools so honored in our system are two of our Early Childhood Centers.

Our progress has been deliberate and carefully planned. It has been accomplished by involving honestly all concerned parties in our thinking and programmatic development, right from the beginning. As a result, we have achieved a collaboration where "ownership" is shared and felt, where enthusiasm and support are almost universal, and where continuous evaluation and modification are seen by all as a normal part of our educational programs. Progress has also been gained by consistently assuring that whatever may have been the immediate cause for change, something educationally significant and exciting would always be waiting "at the end of the bus ride." Even though busing patterns and parental choices would work together to achieve *desegregation*, curriculum programs and careful teacher planning could work toward student and community *integration*. We have worked to assure that strong multicultural emphases throughout the curriculum would not be viewed as appendages to the "really important stuff," but could be seen and understood as integral to the most basic goals of our school system.

Finally, our progress and growth have been achieved by answering the fundamental question of curriculum planning—how much of what kind of learning is required to get where—in concrete and comprehensive ways: taking advantage of and adapting exemplary programs that have proven effective; paying careful attention to strong and exciting beginnings for our youngest students; assuring them of foundations that will, in fact, reduce the chance of later dropout and establish a solid core of academic basics. All of this is planned and attempted in such a manner that a vision of the future guides our decisions—and an accounting of our actions shows that we are working to provide for each student a lifetime of possibilities.

Notes

1   Research shows that high-quality early childhood programs have significant, long-term effects on the lives of children. An eighteen-year study (David P. Weikart, A. S. Epstein, Lawrence J. Schweinhart, and J. T. Bond, *The Ypsilanti Preschool Curriculum Demonstration Project: Preschool Years and Longitudinal Results*. Monographs of the High/Scope Educational Research Foundation, No. 4 [Ypsilanti, Mich.: High/Scope Press, 1978], Tables 1-4), by High/Scope Educational Research Foundation shows that for every $1,000 spent on preschool programs, $4,130 has been or will be returned to society. Children with preschool experience exhibit a 61 percent reduction in numbers needing special education and a 23 percent reduction in numbers retained in grade. All-day programs, in particular, offer major advantages. Increased time in class affords expanded opportunities for acquiring formal and informal learning skills and for enrichment activities. Screening of children coming into the program provides early identification of needs, strengths, and learning styles; it can also fulfill state and national screening requirements. The probability of successful achievement in later grades is enhanced by increased attention to individual needs and by carefully planned continuity. This unique design has resulted in many benefits for children, parents, community, and staff. Parents know that their child's instructional program will continue on an appropriate level without interruption. Expertise and care given to each child's individual instructional profile is a justification for the high level of parent confidence in the Early Childhood Center Program.

2   Tools used in this endeavor include:

The Early Childhood Connection Storyteller: A telephone tape line is prepared each week presenting stories, poems, and nursery rhymes. Children are encouraged to call and listen, then retell the story to someone in the home. This helps to build sequencing skills as well as a positive attitude toward reading. The Early Childhood Connection Storyteller line averages 2,000 calls a month.

The Early Childhood Connection Homework Calendar: Activities are planned as an extension and outgrowth of the program, placed in a calendar format, and delivered to parents. Teachers coordinate class activities with the calendar ideas, and parents follow up at home. Once again, this serves to strengthen the educational bond between home and school.

Other parent-oriented activities include plant sales, assembly programs, Grandparents' Day, and reading days. Formal parent–teacher conferences take place at least twice a year.

The Consequences of Employer Involvement in Child Care

RENÉE YABLANS MAGID
Beaver College, Glenside, Pennsylvania

After tracing the changing forms of work, family life, and child care in America, Magid explores the benefits to family, home life, work place, parents, children, and child care workers afforded by a variety of current employer practices in child care services and support.

The image of the typical American family has been drastically altered in recent years by the increased participation of women in the work force. No longer can the typical family be envisioned with a male head of household supporting his wife and 2.5 children.[1] Today, more than 70 percent of women between the ages of 25 and 34 are working, and, in almost 68 percent of all two-parent families, both parents work. Seventy percent of all single mothers are in the labor force, and mothers with infants and toddlers make up the fastest growing segment in the labor force.[2] A new image of the American family is emerging. It is one in which women and men are assuming new roles. It is one in which concerns about children and their care are becoming a major social and economic issue.

The changed reality of the contemporary American family has prompted changes in the nature of the employer-employee relationship. Among some of the nation's employers, concern about the current work-family dynamic has been signaled by employer initiatives for child care.[3] Services and support by employers to working parents are being crafted in a variety of ways with varying degrees of success.[4] One would probably argue that any employer initiative for child care that helps working parents to successfully merge the often conflicting worlds of work and family will ultimately be beneficial to children. However, I have elected to narrow the focus to a selective discussion of the benefits of employer initiatives for child care that can directly influence and improve the well-being of children, child-care professionals, employers, and parent-employees.

A brief historical review of American work and family patterns will introduce the discussion. Dividing the information into historical units is an attempt to make this information more manageable. It is not intended to imply that these historical periods are precisely delineated or to ignore the interconnectedness of work and family. The reader may best understand the evolution of employer initiatives for child care and perhaps predict future trends amid the background of work-family relationships of the past. Implications for child care may be drawn from this discussion. The article proceeds with a review of the types of employer-sponsored child-care services currently available, including direct services such as work-site child care and participation in child-care consortia, family day care, school-age child care, and sick-child care programs.[5] The results of an informal survey regarding perceived benefits of these services by parents, children, employers, and child-care professionals will follow. The article concludes with suggestions for further research.

A HISTORICAL PERSPECTIVE ON WORK AND FAMILY IN THE UNITED STATES

Employer initiatives for child care have their roots in the preindustrial period (prior to 1840) when a rural culture predominated and family farms and small shops were the major economic units. The work-family relationship in preindustrial America was one of "shared experience," an integrated whole, in which all family members capable of work participated in production and shared in the care and nurturing of the young. No great antagonism, reports Coles, existed between work and family.[6] This prevailing attitude influenced the actions and attitudes of family members toward the balance of work life and family life. Adults and children worked side by side, and children were considered "a social fact not a social problem."[7] Preindustrial work and family life provided numerous opportunities for children to be in close association with a variety of adults, thereby creating an intergenerational bond within families. Work and family in preindustrial America did not constitute two separate worlds as is the case today.

Between 1840 and 1919, three significant phenomena — industrialization, urbanization, and immigration — effected profound changes in the work–family relationship.[8] As centers of production moved from the family farms and small shops in rural areas to factories in the growing cities, a division between work and family life emerged.[9] No longer was the home the center of work: Men went away from home to earn a living. Women's activities were increasingly confined to child care and homemaking. Separation within families took place: children from parents, husbands from wives, and aging parents from adult children. This physical separation of family members along with a division of labor unknown in earlier times gave birth to the notions of family and the role of women that have, until very recently, been considered "traditional."[10]

With the transfer of work from the smaller family enterprise to larger and more impersonal organizations, families began to look to employers not merely for economic support but also for services previously provided within the context of the rural community. Employers, in turn, saw a need to socialize farm workers into different life and work styles and to Americanize a large immigrant population. Out of these shared needs of employers and employees emerged a system of "welfare capitalism," which was evident in the provision of housing, medical care, recreation services, religious facilities, counseling services, and food for workers and their families. In some places, child-care services, such as day nurseries for infants, and educational services, such as primary schools and adult education classes, were also provided.[11]

For economic reasons, immigrant families were by far the largest users of day nurseries. The prevailing societal attitude toward such child-care services was that child care outside the home by someone other than a mother or close family member represented a deficit, a welfare service. These pioneering efforts on behalf of the children of working mothers were viewed as a "relief service" in times of great need or crisis, a temporary service to repair breakdowns when all else had failed, not a service available on a regular and sustained basis. There was general concern that the involvement of social, political, and economic institutions in such family matters might cause the "demise of the American family," with little recognition of the strains on families created by the effort of trying to maintain their equilibrium while adjusting to new modes of living in industrialized urban centers and working in large and impersonal surroundings.

World War I and the period of the Depression saw the demise of welfare capitalism. In a failing labor market and in an environment of large-scale financial and social problems, employers could no longer continue to provide extra support or services to families.[12] The private sector looked to local, state, and federal government to provide relief to families the extent that, by the end of the Depression, the U.S. government had become the primary provider of benefits and services to families.

During the Depression, the federal government gave attention to the financing of nursery schools under a program known as the Works Progress Administration (WPA).[13] The program's primary purpose was to provide employment, mostly for men.[14] However, what emerged were superb child-care programs that have continued to serve as models for child care in the United States. The WPA program set the precedent for public funding of child care and established a government role in the education and guidance of young children.[15]

As families struggled with the changes and conflicts of a major war and a great depression, sporadic attempts at employer-sponsored child care were reported.[16] For the most part, these programs were isolated attempts to meet the needs of poor families in crisis. Thus, the notion of family support as welfare and/or emergency relief was, once again, sustained.

The American family changed greatly during the period of World War I and its aftermath. The world was changing. There was increased separation within families with less time for enjoyment together in work and family activities and a reduction in the time that men spent helping to shape the lives of their children. Increasingly, the role of women was understood to center on the home, where they were to provide devoted care to their children.[17]

World War II saw a temporary reversal in thinking and attitudes about the interrelationship of work and family, as Rosie the Riveter filled the jobs left by tens of thousands of G.I. Joes who had been recruited to fight a major war. Women entered the labor force in record numbers. They proved to be competent in jobs traditionally held by men, and the work place responded by setting up child-care facilities.[18] The conclusion of the war saw the end of popular support for child care and brought the cry "Mothers return home."[19] Many women, however, did not return to the role of homemaker, for they had experienced a new work ethic and a new independence. While the nation had a desire to return to "normalcy," women discovered that working *and* parenting were possible if their work away from home did not interfere with work at home. In an earlier work, I noted that the seeds for "Super Person" were sown during this period in American history.[20]

The ideal of the typical American family was fashioned during the postwar period of the 1950s. After sustained periods of separation, isolation, and emotional starvation fueled by two world wars, a depression, and vast changes in family life, there was a need for American families to attempt to recapture and recreate a romanticized past in which family was dominant. This social ideal was one that popularized middle-class values; "having it all" meant that fathers would work long hours, and mothers would keep the home running like a "well-oiled machine."

The period of the Great Society, 1960–1974, heralded changes in the family as well as in society as a whole. This period was sparked by what Kerr refers to as a "youthful almost warrior like sense of idealism and commitment to social change."[21] A patchwork of programs was fashioned during this period in response to the needs of welfare recipients and the working poor, including Head Start, Follow Through, and a host of antipoverty programs. Past conceptions of family support and child care were reinforced as, once again, child welfare was seen as an effort at remediation for deprived children and their families.[22] The path toward the integration of work and family during this era was one of one step forward and two steps backward. Attempts to provide direct child-care services and support to parents were often piecemeal. However, employer-sponsored child-care centers within health-care organizations, government agencies, and the private sector were emerging.[23]

The period of the 1960s to the early 1970s is often referred to as a revolutionary decade in the history of the American family. It was marked by the emergence of the women's movement and of new values concerning what individuals were calling "job satisfaction."[24] Both men and women were eager to enrich their lives through meaningful work and parenting—the "People's Agenda," as Krepps describes it because the issues surrounding work and family commanded the attention of males and females.[25] Children in the Great Society were incorporated into new family structures. By the mid to late 1970s, the "typical" American family was fading from the American family portrait.

Hermann Hesse has reflected that there are times when a generation is caught between two ages or two modes of life, a circumstance leading to loss of power to understand itself.[26] Hesse could have been describing contemporary American society, in which families appear to be caught between two ways of life: Men and women have abandoned or exchanged traditional roles; today, more parents, both men and women, are in the work force than at any time in history; more than half of the women living in families are now employed outside the home; one out of nine working mothers is the sole support of her family; and more employees report that they want their company to do something about their problems, concerns, and complaints.[27]

Friedman suggests that with more parents at work, their needs will play a significant role as employers attempt to maintain a talented and stable work force.[28] It seems that what employers must do is learn from the past and plan for a future in which the needs of the individual and family can be made more harmonious with those of the work place.

WHAT HISTORY CAN TEACH US

It is obvious that neither the work place nor the family is static. In this century, there has been a radical shift in the types of work people do and the ways in which they attempt to balance their work and family life. The American work place has undergone two significant transitions: (1) from an agricultural base to an industrial base, and (2) from an industrial base to an information-processing and service base.[29] The shift away from the home as the center of work and family life created a tension between work and family that remains with us to this day. It has had a profound impact on the roles of women and men and has fueled debate on society's responsibility toward its young. Support services that were once inherent in the structure of the family and community are no longer available. Increasingly, support is being sought from government and from private employers, and, increasingly, economic considerations have shaped the extent and types of services provided.

During the industrialization of the American work place and during times of crisis, such as the world wars and the Great Depression, family support services were provided by government and employers to accommodate working parents and those in dire need. Today, the demand for family support has grown to encompass middle-income dual-career families and single-parent families. No longer are income, educational level, or national emergency the criteria for determining need. A changing society that has successfully separated work and family life has made the provision of family-support services a prudent element of an employment package. It has also made family-support services good sense and good politics.

With the vast economic and social changes affecting the family and the work place, it has become increasingly clear that a complex, interactive relationship exists between work and family life, worker and work place, the health of the corporation and the well-being of the community. History suggests that changes in the work place have been reflected by changes in family structure. Today, however, we may be witnessing a reversal of this trend: It seems that now the needs of families and of society for a stable work force and an educated populace are pushing the work place toward accommodation to family and partnership with parents. Policy change of this magnitude requires resourcefulness and creativity by both government and private employers. The need is for services that address the concerns of parents of whatever income and educational level for quality care for their children and for work environments that accommodate family considerations.

EMPLOYER INVOLVEMENT IN CHILD-CARE SERVICES

A number of recent studies have investigated employer involvement in work-family issues examining the broad spectrum of employer options for child care along with various plans and solutions that have been implemented.[30] Currently, employers are providing services and support for child care in a number of different ways, including work-site child care, sick-child care, after-school care, reimbursement or subsidies to cover part or all of the cost of child care at other sites, and support of already existing child-care facilities. There are problems inherent in employer involvement in child-care services. These include cost, liability concerns, a growing need for child-care professionals, administrative responsibilities, and problems unique to specific companies and/or specific locations.[31] However, employers who have supported child-care programs, either through direct services or other involvement, have found them to be broadly beneficial.[32]

Using available research on employer-sponsored child-care and data gathered through informal discussions with working parents and child-care professionals, I have tried to assess the outcomes of direct services and support of child care for children, families, employers, and child-care professionals, seeking to ascertain their impact on perceptions of work-family relationships.

PERCEIVED BENEFITS TO EMPLOYERS

Clearly, the marketplace requires that employers operate their businesses at an optimum level of productivity in order to assure profits. A good work environment, employee satisfaction, and the ability to attract and retain a stable, talented work force are essential elements of successful, productive business. More than ever before, today's employers are coming to understand that employee satisfaction and retention are directly linked to work-family issues and that employer involvement in the provision of family-support services has direct and positive outcomes. Among these beneficial outcomes are lower rates of tardiness and absenteeism, especially in settings where sick-child care programs are supported; high morale and loyalty to the organization; improved ability to recruit and retain employees, resulting in significant reduction of costs associated with employee turnover; and earlier return to the work place by employees who take parental leave. Employers have also found that the provision of family-support services has led to greater self-reliance among employees, thereby lessening the "welfare relief" mentality that is contraindicated for the productive work place.[33]

PERCEIVED BENEFITS TO EMPLOYEES

Today's families do not enjoy the informal child-care arrangements of the past. Instead, many working parents must use a "mix" of formal and informal child-care arrangements, which can be both emotionally and financially taxing. Parent–employees who work for organizations that have initiated direct child-care services and/or support for child care report less conflict over feelings of obligation to family and to work. They feel more secure about their children's care, and this translates into greater productivity and improved attitudes toward work and the work place. Parents who travel to work with their children have the added benefit of more time with the children. Parents whose children are nearby clearly are able to respond quickly in child-care emergencies.[34]

PERCEIVED BENEFITS TO CHILD-CARE PROFESSIONALS

Traditionally, child-care professionals have been among the lowest-paid workers in the nation. Thus, the child-care field has been unable to attract and retain the numbers of highly skilled professionals needed. Through the provision of higher salaries and improved working conditions for child-care workers, organizations providing direct employer services and support for child care are helping to change the field. Improved program quality and improved status have brought qualified personnel into the field and resulted in greater professionalism among child-care workers. Child-care environments in which salaries and working conditions are good are marked by high mo-

rale and staff stability. In settings in which parents and child-care professionals share the same employer, there is often a sense of community in which
a "family atmosphere and attitudes prevail."[35]

PERCEIVED BENEFITS TO CHILDREN

Our review of the history of work–family relationships indicates that many
families have been influenced by the notion that nonparental care of children
has a negative effect. In recent years debate has raged over working mothers
and the impact of their employment on their children. The nature of the debate has changed, however. It is no longer about whether care outside the
home is good or bad, for mothers who work outside the home appear to be
here to stay; rather, the debate now concerns the extent to which diminished
parental influence can be offset by quality care.

Unfortunately, today's "children of child care" cannot speak for themselves. The responses of working parents and child-care professionals must
be used to provide information about children served by employer involvement in child care. They report that because these children have more opportunities for interaction with a variety of adults and other children, they
appear to be more independent. Children who have frequent access to parents during the day or whose parents are nearby seem relaxed and secure.
Child-care environments with a professional staff are more likely to provide
children with age-appropriate activities that enhance the social, emotional,
physical, and cognitive development of the child in a daily structure that is
in accord with the elements of child's life space.[36]

CONCLUSION

As the history of child-care services in the United States has shown, society
has rarely recognized the need for the merger of work away from home and
family life. Working parents, specifically women, have usually entered the
labor force without the support of political, social, or economic institutions.
If, as Naisbitt says, the most reliable way to anticipate the future is by understanding the present, then perhaps a prediction for the next decade will be
that we will witness the emergence of family-responsive policies and practices
within most, if not all, U.S. social institutions.[37] As noted earlier, a small
but expanding group of organizations is providing direct child-care services
and support to working parents and making a difference to the health of their
companies, the lives of their parent–employees, and the lives of children.
These employers are helping to create an environment in which business and
families can thrive. If American business is going to enjoy economic survival
in a burgeoning global economy, it must recognize the importance of its social responsibility to help create a balance between work and family life. The

vision of a successful corporate America must embrace social as well as economic goals.

A future research agenda must include information about what families need to successfully merge the worlds of work and family. Data are needed that can satisfy American business that a positive cost–benefit ratio results from this merger. Most important, more research must be done on the effects on children of employer involvement in work-family issues.

I believe that ultimately the implementation of family-responsive policies and practices will have a beneficial effect on the American society of the future.

Notes

1   U.S. Department of Labor, Report of the Secretary's Task Force, *Child Care: A Workforce Issue* (Washington, D.C.: U.S. Government Printing Office, 1988), p. 8.

2   Ibid., pp. 7–8.

3   Renée Y. Magid, *Child Care Initiatives for Working Parents: Why Employers Get Involved* (New York: American Management Association, 1983), pp. 12–13.

4   Ibid., pp. 37–45.

5   For purposes of this report, the definitions of direct employer responses for child care are:

Work-site child care: Services provided by the employer at or in close proximity to the employee's workplace. Also referred to in the literature as "on-site" or "off-site" child care.

Child care consortium: Group of employers who work together to develop and support a parent–employee child care program.

Family day care home: Service that provides care for one to five children of varying ages in the caregiver's home, emphasizing the developmental needs in the natural setting of a family. This is currently the main source of licensed care for infants and toddlers.

School-age child care: For children old enough to attend school and held during those hours school is not in session, such as in the early mornings, late afternoons, on holidays, and during vacation times.

Sick-child care: Care for the mildly ill child when he is not well enough to attend a regularly scheduled program.

6   Robert Coles, "Work and the Family," in *Families and Work: Traditions and Transitions* (Washington, D.C.: American Association of University Women, 1982), pp. 4–5.

7   Carl N. Degler, *At Odds: Women and the Family in America from the Revolution to the Present* (New York: Oxford University Press, 1980), p. 137.

8   Marianne Ferber and Bonnie Bernbaum, "The Impact of Mother's Work on the Family as an Economic System," in *Families That Work: Children in a Changing World*, ed. Sheila B. Kamerman and Cheryl D. Hayes (Washington, D.C.: National Academy Press, 1982), pp. 84–135.

9   Helen Lewis, "Rural Families," in *Families and Work*, pp. 37–38.

10   Degler, *At Odds*, p. 162.

11   Sheila B. Kamerman and Paul W. Kingston, "Employer Responses to the Family Responsibilities of Employees," in *Families That Work*, pp. 144–204. *Note*:   Welfare capitalism is defined as "any service provided for the comfort and improvement of employees which was neither a necessity nor industry or required by law" (p. 151).

12 Ibid., p. 153.

13 Margaret Steinfels, *Who's Minding the Children? The History and Politics of Day Care in America* (New York: Simon & Schuster, 1973), p. 66.

14 Ibid., p. 67.

15 Ibid., p. 68.

16 Virginia Kerr, "One Step Forward, Two Steps Backward in Child Care's Long American History," in *Child Care: Who Cares*, ed. Pamela Roby (New York: Basic Books, 1973), pp. 85–89.

17 Ibid.

18 Ibid.

19 Renée Y. Magid, *When Mothers and Fathers Work: Creative Strategies for Balancing Career and Family* (New York: American Management Association, 1987), p. 52.

20 Ibid., p. 28.

21 Kerr, *One Step Forward*, p. 90.

22 Ibid.

23 Katherine Senn-Perry, "Survey and Analyses of Employer-Sponsored Day Care in the United States," (Ph.D. diss., University of Wisconsin, 1978), pp. 100–10.

24 John Fernandez, *Child Care and Corporate Productivity: Resolving Family Work Conflicts* (Lexington, Mass.: Lexington Books, 1984), p. 8.

25 Juanita Krepps, "The People's Agenda," in *Families and Work*, p. 3.

26 Hermann Hesse, *Steppenwolf*, trans. Basil Crighton, updated by Joseph Mileck (New York: Bantam Books, 1969).

27 Halcyone H. Bohen, *Corporate Employment Policies Affecting Families and Children: The United States and Europe* (New York: Aspen Institute for Humanistic Studies, 1983), pp. 11–36.

28 Dana Friedman, *Encouraging Employer Supports to Working Parents: Community Strategies for Change* (New York: Carnegie Corporation of New York, 1983), p. 7.

29 Sandra Burud et al., *Employer Supported Child Care: Investing in Human Resources* (Boston: Auburn House, 1984); Fernandez, *Child Care and Corporate Productivity*; Friedman, *Encouraging Employer Supports*; Magid, *Child Care Initiatives*; and Senn-Perry, "Survey and Analyses of Employer-Sponsored Day Care."

30 John Naisbitt and Patricia Aburdene, *Reinventing the Corporation: Transforming Your Job and Your Company for the New Information Society* (New York: Warner Books, 1985).

31 Burud et al., *Employer Supported Child Care*; Fernandez, *Child Care and Corporate Productivity*; Friedman, *Encouraging Employer Supports*; Magid, *Child Care Initiatives*; and Senn-Perry, "Survey and Analyses of Employer-Sponsored Day Care."

32 Burud et al., *Employer Supported Day Care*, p. 245.

33 Magid, *Child Care Initiatives*, pp. 38–40.

34 Barbara Adolf and Karol Rose, *The Employers Guide to Child Care* (New York: Praeger, 1985), p. 109.

35 Sally Provence et al., *The Challenge of Day Care* (New Haven: Yale University Press, 1977), pp. 9–10.

36 Information collected by Renée Y. Magid in interview with child care professionals.

37 Naisbitt and Aburdene, *Reinventing the Corporation*.

Self-reflection as an Element
of Professionalism

BARBARA T. BOWMAN

The Erikson Institute, Chicago

Bowman argues that a blend of scientific and personal knowledge is essential for sound professional practice in early childhood education. She emphasizes the need for empathy, subjective understanding, compassion, feeling, and self-knowledge in the professional education of reflective practitioners.

In recent years increasing attention has been devoted to the advantages of professionalizing teaching so that it can enjoy the status and autonomy of the other learned professions.[1] Professionalization has been seen as a way to identify, improve, and protect the quality of teaching practices and as the basis for increased status and wages for teachers. These benefits are particularly compelling for teachers of young children and have given impetus to a movement to professionalize the field of early childhood education.

One of the most important attributes of a profession is that it have a coherent knowledge base. The discussion about the best base for early childhood education has been lively, but has primarily focused on the formal knowledge system — the theories, experiments, and statistical evidence that have served as the basis for practice.[2] Less attention has been given to subjective or personal knowledge as a foundation for teaching. Along with many early childhood educators, I contend that the theoretical underpinning for early childhood education must not be restricted to externally validated knowledge. A number of years ago, I outlined the Erikson Institute's approach to teacher education.[3] The institute's position is that the teaching/learning paradigm is best understood by taking into account personal as well as empirical knowledge. Teachers filter formal theories and ideas regarding practices through their own values, beliefs, feelings, and habits, sometimes expanding and changing their personal knowledge to accommodate new ideas and new experiences, sometimes restructuring it to fit their current needs.

There is no inherent contradiction in having two knowledge systems for teaching: a formal one that includes information about human beings, and a subjective one that includes experiential knowledge of self and others.

Early childhood education has a rich history of valuing the second type of knowledge,[4] and I shall refer to many of the proponents of this point of view in this article. During the past twenty to thirty years the objective sciences — the formal knowledge system — have occupied the attention of early childhood educators. There is some reason to believe that the pendulum swing of theory and research is ready to move back once more to an appreciation of the relationship of personal experience and feelings to ideas and behavior.[5]

What is personal knowledge and is it respectable enough to be considered professional? It is not as easily described and examined as is formal knowledge, and teachers themselves are often poor guides to it, showing inconsistencies and disagreement between their expressed ideas and their feelings, between their formally stated beliefs and their actions in their classrooms. Yet it is this "implicitly held knowledge"[6] that undergirds teachers' actions.

Reflection has been recognized as a useful technique for helping teachers integrate the scientific and personal knowledge systems.[7] It is assumed that if teachers reflect on their practices, they can make their understanding of classroom events more explicit, and therefore more amenable to control and direction. Teachers who reflect on how they feel and why they feel the way they do are in a better position to understand their interactions with others. The purpose of this article is to point out how professional practice is enhanced by self-reflection.

REFLECTION TO UNDERSTAND HOW CHILDREN FEEL

Barbara Biber, in *Early Education and Psychological Development*, describes a scene from her childhood to exemplify her school experience. Now in her eighties, Biber writes about the New York City schools of the early 1900s and of one of her first teachers. This teacher was prone to loud and histronic outbursts in class. One day, before the class began, Biber did an imitation of her teacher to entertain the other children. What she did not realize was that the teacher was in the cloakroom listening. The teacher's response to Biber's childhood prank was so painful that she still remembered it more than a half a century later. The teacher called her a bad girl, and moved her to a seat directly in front of the teacher. Biber says that this experience made a lasting impression on her and affected her feelings about school.[8]

Biber's remembrance struck an empathic chord in me because I had a similar experience. Mine happened in nursery school. My first memory is of noticing that my snow suit was around my ankles and that something was not quite right. I evidently realized as I was tugging away that my suit was on back to front. For some reason I elected to pull the suit on, put my arms in, and present myself to the teacher. I do not know what I expected but my teacher responded, "Look at Barbara, she can't even put her snow suit on right." She then zipped me up the back. Biber's story brought this event back to me. Shock, outrage, and shame are as clear now as when it happened.

The ability of humans to connect their experience to that of others, and through that connection gain understanding of the feelings of others, is a vital component of interpersonal interaction. The empathic capacity to feel with others, to sense the personal feelings of another, is at the heart of human understanding. Empathy is critical if adults are really to understand young children. Anna Freud has said, "We have, indeed, to rely upon the capacity of the normal adult to remember things, upon his interest in the investigation and upon his willingness to overthrow all those barriers, erected by a sense of shame, which prevent the revelation of himself to others."[9] It is through the teacher's own prior experience, intuitive human knowledge, and subjective understanding that a great deal about the child is revealed.

Understanding the meaning of experience for young children is so important because some of their memories will be lifelong ones and will affect how later experiences are interpreted. The great black poet Countee Cullen wrote:

Once traveling in old Baltimore
   Heart-filled, head filled with glee
   I saw a Baltimorean
   Kept looking straight at me

   Now I was eight and very small
   and he was no whit bigger
   And so I smiled but he poked out
   His tongue and called me nigger

   I saw the whole of Baltimore
   From May until December
   Of all the things that happened there
   That's all that I remember[10]

Teachers may overlook childhood pain if they have not been sensitized through reflection on their own childhood and its pain. Access to these feelings is an important dimension of teachers' self-knowledge and an asset in understanding their students and interactions with them. Sykes contends that the ethos of science-driven practice encourages detached personal relationships between the worker and the client, resulting in less sensitive and compassionate interactions.[11]

Nancy Balaban says in the dedication of her book *Starting School*, "When my youngest daughter went to kindergarten an event took place that caused her daily distress. The teacher, it seems, put Willie in the coat room every morning because he cried for his mother. He was permitted back in the classroom when he stopped crying. Eventually he learned not to cry for his mother." Balaban goes on to say, "This book is written in the belief that other solutions to Willie's crying can be found."[12] Teachers may ask, why worry about another solution? Willie stopped crying. Was it not good for him to learn he could not disrupt the class? The teacher's idea of success might have changed if she had reflected. Balaban reports that when she conducted workshops with teachers and got them to think of words they associated with separation, they listed such feelings as fear, anxiety, pain, alone, angry, out of control, help, and unhappy. They had clear memories of the pain that can accompany separation.[13]

Teachers create emotionally stressful experiences for children, perhaps because they do not remember their own childish passions, misunderstandings, and errors in judgment. Reflection on their own personal past can break teachers' concentration on formal goals and objectives and focus attention on children's "gut-level" experience. When teachers recognize at a personal level how a child may feel, they are more willing to take his or her feelings seriously and make supportive arrangements. Whether the teacher sees a child's crying as behavior to be ignored or as an indication of pain to which he or she should respond depends on the meshing of personal and formal knowledge. Basch summarizes well when he notes that empathy leads to knowledge.[14]

Painful experiences do not have to constrain the rest of a child's life. Adults can buffer children's experience so that potentially devastating events become facilitating and growth producing instead of constricting and regressive. Some of the experiences that are apt to cause lifelong painful memories for children are well known—the death of someone important, rejection by a loved one, and violence are almost always traumatic. There are other experiences that stand out as strongly for young children, experiences like the first day in school, failing a test, or being called "nigger." By remembering their own needs and vulnerabilities during childhood, teachers can learn to recognize when children are struggling with an experience and need help. They can then give comfort and support and teach children effective strategies for coping.

It is not just with strong emotions that memories can help teachers better understand children. Teachers' memories help them to understand children's sensory experience. Teachers who do not permit themselves to remember and still enjoy the texture of sense experiences, who are unable to reestablish their connectedness to the feelings of their own childhood, will not grasp the significance of sense experiences for children. Teachers who retain their own joy in the senses can use their knowledge to plan curriculum for children.

REFLECTION TO UNDERSTAND ONESELF

The responsiveness of the young child to adult perceptions and expectations is well known to teachers in relation to parents. Teachers usually see the relationship between parents' behavior and attitudes and a child's feelings, but often are less sensitive to their own effect on children. They are less willing to see how their past experiences and present concerns affect children's feelings and behavior. Requiring teachers to look inward at themselves, at their fears, anxieties, disappointments — even looking inward on what makes them happy or satisfied — can make them uncomfortable. People create defenses against knowing about themselves when self-knowledge is too painful. Is it fair to ask teachers to put themselves in the position of feeling personal discomfort or pain? Yes. Is it not enough for them to just do the job? No. Should their personal lives be involved in their work? Yes.

This was brought home to me while observing a teacher trying to teach young children a unit about sexual abuse. The teacher abruptly told the children that there is "good touching" and "bad touching," without making clear what makes a touch good or bad. Her hurried and embarrassed presentation made clear her discomfort with the topic. Many adults in our society feel uncomfortable about the fact that young children have and enjoy genital stimulation, with the fact that children are sexual beings. Much adult discomfort is caused by guilt and shame residual from their own childish sexual interests or activities. The teacher I observed was unable to discuss sexuality with the children because her feelings got in the way, and her lesson served little purpose. When teachers are able to admit to and discuss their feelings, shame and guilt may be relieved through the recognition of the universality of these childhood feelings.

Teachers can also gain valuable understanding of a child's problems by attending to the feelings that the child evokes in them. Children often behave in ways that provoke adults to validate the child's understanding of the world. For instance, children who have experienced abusive relationships with adults may be extremely provocative, trying to prove their wickedness or to duplicate the earlier relationship. Teachers who deny the anger and rage the child's provocativeness elicits lose the insight into the child's issues that knowing their feelings can reveal. Similarly, children having difficulty with establishing a clear and separate identity may hang on the teacher constantly. Teachers who do not recognize the discomfort this clinging makes them feel may reject the child's overtures without insight into the cause of the child's behavior.

Conflicts between formal and personal knowledge frequently go undetected because of the tacit nature of the latter. These conflicts can be addressed if teachers' past experiences, their residual affects, are articulated and made respectable components of professional knowledge. Self-reflection and self-knowledge can be antidotes to exploitive and callous relationships.

TEACHERS AS MODELS FOR CHILDREN

Teachers who recognize and accept their feelings as part of a legitimate knowledge system set a good example for children. Two of the criteria for staff-child interactions of the National Association for the Education of Young Children's Center Accreditation Project are "Staff help children deal with anger, sadness, and frustration" and "Children are encouraged to talk about feelings."[15] There is no better way of learning about feelings than having adults model for children. Children will learn about the importance of their inner selves through interaction with adults who recognize the importance of their inner selves and by identifying with those adults. Barbara Merril says in *Learning about Teaching from Children*, "All day, every day, the children study the behavior of the people who care for them, and learn to talk that way to one another and to us."[16]

Learning to talk about feelings with young children is not always easy. Sometimes the reasons for adult feelings are beyond the understanding of a young child, as when adults are disappointed in love or scared of losing a job. Self-reflection coupled with good supervision and team work can inform teachers when they are not being good models for children; colleagues can take over for the teacher when feelings get out of hand and the teacher can no longer control them; they can listen as teachers talk through why a particular child is so difficult; and they can reassure a teacher that everyone has feelings that are not helpful to children and that these can be controlled. When teachers recognize the need to support and help one another deal with feelings, they are good models and are being professional.

TEACHER EDUCATION AND PROFESSIONALISM

In 1955, Jersild said that teacher education had hardly begun to explore how to help teachers develop self-knowledge.[17] This is still true today. If one looks at teacher education curricula, one rarely finds much emphasis on self-understanding. Teachers are generally given very little help using reflection and self-knowledge on behalf of children. They do not learn to talk professionally about feelings so that they communicate without invading each other's privacy or exposing more about themselves than they are comfortable telling. The organization of trustworthy environments and the development of professional attitudes about the expression of feelings must be part of the teacher education curriculum.

Elizabeth Jones has described how she arranges a trustworthy environment for her students at Pacific Oaks. Memories from childhood are an integral part of her course in child development as a way of helping teachers discover the essence of childhood. Students are expected to participate in small-group discussions and to prepare journals in which remembrance of feelings is an important component.[18] Through talking with others, teachers can learn to deal with their early experiences — some of which have been painful. Erikson says, "It is in certain phases of his work that the adult projects past experiences into dimensions which seem manageable. In the laboratory, on the stage, and on the drawing board, he relives the past and thus relieves left over affects; in restructuring the model situation, he redeems his failures and strengthens his hopes. He anticipates the future from the point of view of a corrected and shared past."[19] With skilled supervision, teachers can encourage each other to step back from their distinctly personal issues and see the developmental similarity of their own experience with that of others.

The experiences and feelings of childhood endure. Teachers have a responsibility to help shape children's experiences so that they are growth-producing and self-assuring rather than constricting and self-doubting. Learning to use self-reflection to improve teaching deserves greater attention than it is currently receiving. By helping teachers get in touch with their own feelings, both past and present, another dimension of knowledge is activated, a dimension that should have a high priority in the profession of teaching. At the same time that this dimension of knowledge is more fully recognized in teacher education, it can be articulated with the existing formal knowledge base, so that the two together can form the coherent base to ground and shape future practice in the care and education of young children. Reflection, again, is the key to the process.

Notes

1　Walter Metzer, "A Spectre Haunts American Scholars: The Spectre of 'Professionalism'," in *Educational Researcher* 19, no. 6 (August–September 1987): 10–18.

2　"The Most Important Principle for Early Childhood Teacher Preparation Is . . ." (Panel presentation at the National Association for the Education of Young Children Annual Meeting, Chicago, November 13, 1987).

3　Barbara T. Bowman, *Proceedings from the National Symposium on Teaching and Learning* (Urbana-Champaign: College of Education, University of Illinois at Urbana-Champaign, 1977), pp. 30–33.

4　Arthur Jersild, *When Teachers Face Themselves* (New York: Bureau of Publications, Teachers College, Columbia University, 1955); and Barbara Biber and Vera Bernard, *Teacher Education in Mental Health* (New York: Bank Street College of Education, 1967).

5　Jacqueline Goodnow, "Parents' Ideas, Actions, and Feelings: Models and Methods from Developmental and Social Psychology," in *Child Development* 59, no. 2 (April 1988): 286–320.

6　Margaret Yonemura, *A Teacher at Work* (New York: Teachers College Press, 1986), p. 6.

7　Kenneth Zeichner and Daniel Liston, "Teaching Student Teachers to Reflect," *Harvard Educational Review* 57, no. 2 (February 1987): 23–48.

8　Barbara Biber, *Early Education and Psychological Development* (New Haven: Yale University Press, 1984).

9　Anna Freud, *Psychoanalysis for Teachers and Parents* (Boston: Beacon Press, 1963), p. 22.

10　Countee Cullen, "Incident," in his *Color* (New York: Harper & Brothers, 1925), p. 15.

11　Gary Sykes, "Reckoning with the Spectre," *Educational Researcher* 16, no. 6 (August–September 1987): 19–21.

12　Nancy Balaban, *Starting School* (New York: Teachers College Press, 1985), Preface.

13　Ibid., p. 12.

14   Michael S. Basch, "Empathic Understanding: A Review of the Concept and Some Theoretical Considerations," *Journal of Psychoanalytic Association* 31, no. 2 (1983): 101–26.

15   *Accreditations Criteria and Procedures of the National Academy of Early Childhood Programs* (Washington, D.C.: National Association for the Education of Young Children, n.d.).

16   Barbara Merrill, *Learning about Teaching from Children* (Henrieta, N.Y.: Rochester Association for the Education of Young Children, 1984), p. 9.

17   Jersild, *When Teachers Face Themselves*, p. 11.

18   Elizabeth Jones, *Teaching Adults* (Washington, D.C.: National Association for the Education of Young Children, 1986), p. 8.

19   Erik Erikson, *Childhood and Society* (New York: Norton, 1950), p. 195.

Early Childhood in Public Education: Managing Change in a Changing Field

FRANCES O'CONNELL RUST

Manhattanville College, Purchase, New York

Using a case study of a community's reaction to an all-day kindergarten proposal, Rust explores impediments and avenues to educational change along the technical, political, and cultural dimensions. She sees the field of early childhood education at a crossroads, needing to go public and appeal to many constituencies, but perhaps compromising its mission and identity in the process.

Increasingly, school systems around the country are considering the adoption of early childhood programs. These range from all-day kindergarten to day care and include programs for four-year-olds, teen parent centers with care for young children, infant and toddler programs, and other services for preschoolers and their families. Whether such programs should come under the purview of school districts is immaterial in this movement. The fact is that it is happening and it has startling implications for the field of early childhood. Policy, leadership, professional preparation, licensing, curriculum, services — all are and will continue to be affected. Early childhood educators need to be concerned about the management of change in their field, for a time of change is upon them. The question is: Will the movement to bring early childhood into the arena of public education strengthen the field as a whole or will it dissipate energies and splinter the field?

This article describes the introduction of an all-day kindergarten program in a small suburban school district. The change process is examined specifically for its implications for adoption and implementation of early childhood programs in other school systems. The article concludes with recommendations for the management of early childhood innovations in public school settings.

THE PROCESS OF CHANGE

Educators have learned a lot about innovation and change in schools over the past twenty years. We know that contextual factors such as history,[1] operational routines, and institutional image[2] are of paramount importance in determining the outcome of an innovation. We have found that change is most productively seen as a social process that gradually unfolds over time.[3] Most important, we have learned that change is not easy to manage: Successful innovations are marked by strong leadership, broad-based commitment, and institutionalization.[4]

Knowledge of the change process can help early childhood educators adapt to changes in the field and enable us to develop, guide, and implement programs in school systems. We are, however, faced with unique problem areas. There are problems in how outsiders — other educators, parents, and society in general — perceive the field of early childhood. We have problems getting ourselves to agree on professional policy and standards of practice. These problems are rather striking when considered against the backdrop of the current movement to incorporate early childhood programs in public education.

A CASE IN POINT

In 1984, I completed a case study of a school district's efforts to develop and implement an all-day kindergarten program.[5] The outcome of this effort was an extended-morning kindergarten — an hour more of kindergarten extending the program from 11:30 to 12:30 — *not* a full-day kindergarten program. Five years later, the district continues to have an extended-morning program. To some in the district, the new program was an instance of successful change because it was new and was in place; to others, it was an instance of failure because they had set out to develop an all-day kindergarten program and ended up with a compromise that added only an hour more to the kindergarten day. For me, the researcher, the outcome had minimal importance in comparison with the rich lessons the innovation effort provided about the integration of early childhood programs in schools, for, in many ways, the story of the effort to change the length of the kindergarten day in Rosedale (a fictitious name) is instructive about the process of initiating and implementing early childhood education innovations in school systems.

Rosedale is a small suburban school district serving twelve hundred students, most of whom are college bound. In 1982, Rosedale, like many school systems around the country, had embarked on a "back-to-basics" regimen: Test scores throughout the district were improving as was management and discipline in the district's three schools. The open-classroom movement of the late 1960s and 1970s was a thing of the past, discernible to newcomers only in the physical design of the district's ten-year-old high school building and in some of the curricular offerings of the elementary school. Rosedale was faced with two major educational decisions: whether to merge with a neighboring district because of declining enrollments, and whether to institute an all-day kindergarten. Both change efforts were initiated at a grass-roots level. Neither was espoused by the district administration or the school board. In the end, neither change was implemented.

The initiative for an all-day kindergarten program came from the only full-time kindergarten teacher, an eight-year veteran of the system and the least senior member of the elementary school staff. She was joined during the spring of 1982 by a small group of kindergarten and elementary school parents who were members of the school's parent-teacher association. Together they approached the elementary school principal, who gave her support to their proposal because she saw in it a way of providing job security for teachers in a period of declining enrollments and she was sensitive to parental pressures for a longer day: Preschoolers in area nursery schools spent more time in their classrooms each day than did children in the Rosedale kindergarten.[6]

This coalition of teacher, principal, and interested parents developed a questionnaire that was sent to the parents of all current and prospective kindergarteners in the district. The questionnaire focused on the preschool experience of prospective kindergarteners and on parental attitudes toward all-day/every-day kindergarten. Because it was the first signal of district interest in all-day kindergarten and because it provided no opportunity for parents to suggest alternate kindergarten arrangements, the questionnaire was unintentionally inflammatory. Within days of its release, the community was engulfed by the kindergarten issue; within a matter of weeks, the issue had polarized the community, with parents and professional educators in conflict over what constituted good education for young children.

Parents who received the questionnaire and many who heard about it assumed that all-day kindergarten was already a *fait accompli*. They were angry that they had not been consulted. Many felt that a full-day/every-day program was inappropriate and unnecessary for their children, and they were concerned about fatigue and academic pressure. While there were many areas of disagreement among the parents during the following year of discussion, study, and implementation of the compromise extended-morning program, they were united in their determination to have a say in the development and implementation of a new kindergarten program in the district.

Like the parents, the professional educators in the district disagreed on a number of substantive issues related to the all-day kindergarten program. The kindergarten teacher and her two part-time colleagues saw it as a way to enhance the kindergarten program by enriching the curriculum and by providing a less pressured environment where children had time to explore new ideas and to work longer on activities of interest to them. The principal saw it as a way to meet parental demands for more time, to retain good teachers in a time of declining enrollments and concomitant staff cutbacks, and to ensure continuity among the kindergarten staff, which she could not do with part-time faculty. In her effort to make the program acceptable to the district administration and the school board, the principal insisted on a rigorous evaluation of the new extended-day program using standardized test scores as evidence of academic improvement. She also insisted on pushing the all-day/every-day format as the only economically feasible option. Both stands were antithetical to those of the kindergarten staff, yet the staff worked within the principal's guidelines and never publicly voiced opposition. The principal, the kindergarten teachers, and the elementary school faculty were united in their belief that all-day kindergarten was a way of saving jobs.

In the fall of 1982, following the publication of the all-day kindergarten questionnaire in Rosedale, a compromise program was implemented: the extended-morning kindergarten. A committee of parents was commissioned by the superintendent of schools and the school board to study all-day kindergarten and to make a recommendation to the school board by March 1983. No teachers or administrators were invited to join this committee. The school board appointed one of its members as liaison. The committee worked throughout the fall reading about, studying, and observing other kindergarten programs. By January, they were developing a preliminary report that was supportive of some type of alternate-day program allowing children to stay for a full day one or two days each week.

During the fall, the kindergarten teacher and the principal worked to develop assessment measures for the extended-morning program. Their work was designed to support their case for a full-day program. By January, they had a new parent questionnaire ready and had begun to develop data on academic performance of children in the program. The principal, meanwhile, was under fire from the school board, which wanted an accounting of the full-time kindergarten teacher's time. From the board's perspective, it appeared that the teacher was doing nothing in the afternoons after the children were dismissed. To placate the board, the principal initiated a modified call-back program for ten at-risk kindergarten children: On two afternoons each week, these children stayed in school and worked with the kindergarten teacher on special activities designed to improve their academic performance.

The initiation of the call-back program at the end of January was the major turning point in the Rosedale kindergarten innovation. Until that time, the possibility of some type of alternate-day arrangement seemed likely: The principal was beginning to revise her notion that the school board would support only a full day/every-day program; the kindergarten teachers were starting to develop curriculum for a longer day; and the kindergarten committee was moving toward closer interaction with the elementary school and toward a recommendation for some type of alternate-day program. By going to the board without consulting with the members of the kindergarten committee, the principal alienated them. The atmosphere was reminiscent of the early days of the innovation, when parents who had not been aware of initiatives to revamp the kindergarten felt that a new program was being forced on them and their children. They responded with hostility.

In February, the principal announced her decision to retire at the end of the 1983 school year. Until this time, she had been the spokesperson for the kindergarten teachers to the administration and the board. Her decision to retire forced these teachers to the forefront of the deliberations about the kindergarten program. In March, the kindergarten teachers received notice that they were to be laid off. At the same time, the kindergarten committee made its recommendation against an all-day program on economic grounds and voted to continue the extended-morning program the following year with three seven-tenths-time kindergarten teachers and three aides. By the end of April, the teachers had been reinstated. In September, one was transferred back to a full-time position in the fourth grade; the other part-time person received a full-time position in the second grade; two new part-time kindergarten teachers were hired; the full-time kindergarten teacher continued in her full-time position.

ANALYSIS

There are a number of aspects of this story that are relevant to the adoption, implementation, and institutionalization of early childhood programs in public schools and to understanding the ways in which early childhood programs may be perceived in school settings.

MOBILIZATION FOR ADOPTION

Studies of educational change identify mobilization as the single most important stage in the change process.[7] This includes identifying the need for change, assessing the political climate, marshaling support especially from the district office,[8] and developing strategies for implementation. Kurt Lewin described mobilization as "unfreezing"—developing new understandings of the innovation and forming new coalitions.[9] It is a process that, when well done, should involve what Seymour Sarason terms "confronting history": exploring individuals' relationships to the setting, "dealing with a history of structural relationships," and using "this historical knowledge for actions which maximize the chances that the new setting will be viable and in ways consistent with its values and goals."[10] Mobilization takes time.

In Rosedale, mobilization was, at best, problematic. In the first place, it was rushed. The lapsed time between the first public mention of all-day kindergarten (in the spring 1982 questionnaire) and the implementation of a new kindergarten schedule was less than eight months. By pushing so quickly for a new program, the principal and teachers cut short the time needed to "unfreeze" and develop new understandings. There were few opportunities for free-ranging discussion and rapprochement; after the January call-back decision, there were none.

It was not just the schedule of the kindergarten innovation that kept the various participants separate. The organizational structure of the Rosedale schools was also an effective deterrent to interaction. Parents, teachers, and administration in Rosedale were guarded with one another and maintained their initial positions on all-day kindergarten throughout the year. For the superintendent, the school board, and some long-time residents of Rosedale, the movement toward all-day kindergarten was economically motivated and was designed to provide child care, not education. It would, they thought, inevitably give the teachers more power and would increase the school budget at a time when fiscal restraint was the watchword of the district. Not only did this group question academic gains claimed for an hour more of school, they also questioned the potential gains generally cited for early childhood interventions. There were overtones to their arguments that suggested that their position was (1) that Rosedale children do not need early intervention programs and (2) that good mothers are those who stay home with their children.

The mobilization process in Rosedale did not enable the participants to "confront [their] history."[11] At the time of the kindergarten innovation, Rosedale was struggling to define a new image for itself away from open education and away from having the highest paid teachers in the area. In this back-to-basics climate, "experiments" such as all-day kindergarten were bound to receive careful scrutiny and to require broad-based support if they were to be successful. The kindergarten teachers and the Rosedale principal seemed unprepared to argue for their program on either academic or economic grounds. They seemed unaware of the fact that their proposal of an all-day kindergarten program in Rosedale challenged deeply held beliefs about child care, good mothering, and the role of schools. They seemed ignorant of the fact that most new programs in the district received district-office support after, not before, they had the general support of the community.

Despite significant problems during the mobilization stage, a new kindergarten program was adopted in Rosedale. It was a compromise developed by the superintendent, who wanted to buy time. The fact that a compromise program was developed and adopted suggests the importance of the issue and the power of professional educators to shape what takes place in schools with or without community support.

IMPLEMENTATION

The implementation stage is that period during which the innovation is decided on, tried, and used in a school. Like mobilization, implementation can take a while. Also like mobilization, the outcomes are not always predictable. We do know that what has taken place in a district and a school during the mobilization phase and the participants' reasons for pursuing the innovation have a profound shaping effect on whether an innovation is adopted and on whether it is used.[12]

School people respond in one of three ways to an innovation: They may simply reject it (nonimplementation); they may make it look like they are using it, but in fact change nothing (cooptation); or they may adopt it, changing it to fit the settings and changing themselves to accommodate to the innovation (mutual adaptation).[13] The complexity of the innovation and the level of teacher involvement are the key indicators of which of these three responses will prevail.

Where teachers have been integral to planning and decision making, prepared to use the innovation, and know they can count on continued support, innovations are adopted. Principal involvement and visibility is essential to implementation not only to provide support but also to advocate for the innovation with new staff, community members, and administration. Another key ingredient for successful implementation is community involvement and support.[14]

Rosedale's extended-morning kindergarten program was a relatively simple innovation—an hour more of school. Because it required minor schedule adjustments, staff changes, and budget increases and no staff development for the kindergarten teachers nor any interactive work across grade levels in the elementary school, it was easily accepted by the district administration. The kindergarten parents had no choice about the program. From their perspective, it was better than the morning/afternoon programs, which required a schedule change midyear, and it did give more time in school. The teachers were not concerned about the program. To them, implementation was fairly straightforward, allowing more time for their work with kindergarten children. It was the kindergarten study committee—specifically the scope of its work and the effect it would have on the kindergarten program—that concerned them.

The major source of resistance to the program came from the principal, who correctly saw that it was not a solution to the problem of staff turnover or staff retention—her reasons for advocating all-day kindergarten. During the year of trial, she continued to press for an all-day program and sought ways to convince the school board and the superintendent that it was the only viable alternative to half-day programs. Her strategies, which included the use of standardized tests and comparisons between earlier kindergarten groups and those in the extended-morning program, were designed to convince the administration of the value of more time. She had not anticipated that her strategies would bring her into conflict with the kindergarten teachers, for whom such measures were antithetical to good teaching as they saw it. Nor did she foresee that by taking the lead in the way that she did, she would exclude the kindergarten teachers from the decision-making process and thus leave them unprepared for the advocacy role into which they were forced by her retirement announcement.

INSTITUTIONALIZATION

Institutionalization is the final phase of the change process. Lewin described it as "refreezing"[15] — the time when the system's use of the innovation becomes fixed as an integral part of the day-to-day operation of the school. The outcome of this phase depends on the way things are done, the degree of commitment from the district (including financial commitment), and the level of involvement of various participants during the mobilization and implementation phases.[16] Berman and McLaughlin found that projects that were institutionalized bore similar characteristics: "They tended to have been successfully implemented, to have produced teacher change, and to be marked by the continued extensive use by teachers of project methods."[17]

The fact that Rosedale continues with an extended-morning program does not signal institutionalization. The changes engendered by this compromise program were minimal. The kindergarten teachers did not develop new curriculum or teaching methods. New staffing arrangements were not tried; neither were cross-grade interactions between teachers. The extended-morning kindergarten enabled the district to preserve the status quo: At minimal expense and with little disruption to the elementary school program, it was able to respond to the parents' and teachers' demands for more time.

PERSPECTIVES TOWARD CHANGE

Increasingly, educational change is understood as a social process in which participants negotiate strategies and outcomes over a period of time.[18] In this process, participants' perspectives or understandings of the problem shape their responses both as individuals and as groups.[19]

In his analysis of studies of educational innovation, Ernest House identifies three perspectives on change — technological, political, and cultural — that encompass the totality of viewpoints on the change process. House defines perspective as a " 'way of seeing' a problem rather than a rigid set of rules and procedures."[20] From the technological perspective, change is "conceived of as a relatively mechanistic process."[21] "From the political perspective, innovation is a matter of conflicts and compromises among factional groups. . . . Cooperation on an innovation is viewed as problematic rather than automatic. Cooperation must result from negotiation and compromise."[22] From the cultural perspective, innovation involves changing beliefs; it is a long, slow process that can take a generation or more. Many studies of educational change, writes House, "show the subtle ways in which change efforts are absorbed without significant change occuring."[23]

House suggests that these perspectives "act as interpretive frameworks for understanding the change process [and] . . . may be considered as 'moral' or 'action' paradigms" guiding participants' response to the change.[24] Successful instances of change, House writes, incorporate all three perspectives: There is a new way of doing things; there has been and often continues to be negotiation; and there is a fundamentally different understanding of the innovation on the part of the participants.[25]

One of the most notable aspects of the innovation process in Rosedale was the inability of the various participant groups to communicate with one another about the kindergarten program on any level other than what House describes as the "technological perspective."[26] The outcome of the process — the recommendation to continue the extended-morning program and to staff it with three part-time teachers — was an operative example of technological innovation. Change at the political level and cultural levels did not take place in Rosedale. There was no provision for negotiation or compromise among the various groups of participants. Within their own groups, teachers, parents, administrators, and the school board talked about child care, early childhood education, and kindergarten curriculum and goals; within these groups, there was disagreement, discussion, and compromise. However, public discussions among the participant groups focused on time, money, staffing, and schedule; these discussions had none of the richness of the intra-group exchanges.

As the year of innovation unfolded, it became ever more clear that the kindergarten issue had touched what House describes as the "cultural perspective"[27] — the most difficult level at which to create change because it involves the "gut" feelings and beliefs of participants. In Rosedale, these operative belief systems included beliefs about good mothering, the role of the school, and images of the good teacher: Good mothers are those who stay home with their young children; schools should not be in the business of providing child care; good teachers are professionals who manage instruction. Because there was no vehicle for discussion and negotiation among the various groups involved in the kindergarten program, participants in Rosedale seem to have remained frozen in their attitudes toward all-day kindergarten and to have been unable to develop the innovation beyond the technological perspective.

The Rosedale kindergarten innovation was neither complex nor broad in scope. It was intended to affect only a few teachers and one grade level of the elementary school. Instead, it involved the entire community and brought to light deep divisions within it that even now, five years later, have not been repaired. The fact that it was an early childhood innovation may have had a lot to do with the controversy it evoked, for early childhood, like teaching, is a field about which many people have very definite opinions.

Early childhood innovations tend to be emotion-laden. They challenge adults' beliefs about childhood and the family.[28]

IMPLICATIONS FOR THE FIELD

While the generalizations that can be drawn from a single instance of change are limited, if they are related to the body of practical and theoretical literature on educational innovation, patterns of broad utility and relevance can be identified.[29] The case of Rosedale has implications for increasing our general understanding of the process of educational change and for managing the adoption, implementation, and institutionalization of early childhood programs in school systems. It provides evidence of the types of difficulties that early childhood innovations in public schools are likely to encounter and suggests that recent statements describing public schools as "having the capacity to develop high-quality early childhood education" because of their "knowledge base about young children" and their "advantage of credibility in the community and well-established connections with parents" may be ill founded.[30]

As the story of the kindergarten innovation in Rosedale suggests, early childhood innovations are likely to challenge the operative norms and beliefs that shape the climate and guide the activities of school systems. On the technological level, they require changes in scheduling, budgeting, staffing, curriculum development, and evaluation methods. On the political level and cultural levels, they affect interactions between teachers, between teachers and administration, and between home and school.

The Rosedale story suggests that the major obstacle to the adoption of early childhood innovations in public schools may not be technological or political; it may be a cultural obstacle and, therefore, very difficult to address. Early childhood innovations tend to touch on participants' beliefs about good mothering, the role of schools, and good teaching. The failure of the all-day kindergarten innovation in Rosedale suggests that the way to handle resistance at the cultural level is not to develop simple technological responses that skirt the issue nor to address beliefs and feelings directly but rather to keep the discussion at the political level, inviting negotiation and compromise. In early childhood innovations this means addressing parental concerns about type of program, fatigue, length of day, curriculum, socialization, and nurture. It means addressing administrative concerns about cost and management. It means focusing the discussion on what a good early childhood program looks like and not on whether to have one. It means starting off with input from the broad spectrum of participants, not just colleagues. Most importantly, it means developing and articulating a sound rationale for early childhood programs that will have credibility to administrators, school boards, and parents.

Early childhood educators operate from a philosophical and professional base that is not altogether congruent with those of most primary and elementary school settings. Traditionally, early childhood programs have existed either outside of or on the periphery (as in the case of kindergarten) of the public schools. Early childhood educators have, therefore, not had to defend their practices to school boards and school administrators. As initiatives to bring early childhood programs into school settings increase, this will change.

The Rosedale kindergarten innovation was an example of the phenomenon of "cooptation . . . in which staff adapt the project, usually emasculating it, to meet their needs, without any corresponding change in traditional institutional behavior or practices."[31] This has happened on a regular basis to early childhood programs, particularly kindergarten, as they have been institutionalized in elementary schools: Generally, there has been a tendency for them to lose their early childhood identity and to adopt the instructional practices and curriculum of the elementary school, particularly first-grade reading and whole-group instruction.

Among kindergarten teachers, a similar and in some ways more subtle transformation has taken place. Those who have been transferred into the kindergarten from upper grades, as were two of the three teachers in Rosedale, bring with them the instructional practices and professional ethos of the elementary school. Rarely are they provided with the intensive, ongoing staff development that would enable them to adapt their instruction to work with young children. Those who were prepared as early childhood educators, like the full-time teacher in Rosedale, often find themselves without peer support for the uncomplicated, direct, and highly interactive work they are accustomed to performing in most early childhood settings. In an effort to "fit in" with the other teachers in the school, they often adopt the educational jargon, instructional practices, and professional demeanor and dress of their elementary colleagues. They thus distance themselves from parents, who, in early childhood settings, are their primary sources of support.

If these trends are to change and if early childhood programs coming into public schools are to retain their identity, early childhood educators and change agents will have to become effective advocates for their programs. They will need to interface with fellow educators, administrators, and school boards. This may mean becoming more familiar with current educational research in areas that pertain to the field: curriculum and teaching, learning styles, evaluation methods, and educational change. It may also mean adopting a more assertive professional stance that will give them a voice in decision making about and management of early childhood programs in schools.

The field of early childhood is at a crossroad. The movement to bring early childhood programs into public schools could result in a loss of identity for the field as practitioners try to fit themselves and their programs into settings that are not congruent with the philosophy and practices of the field. Or, it could result in a strengthening of the field as the knowledge base of the field and standards of professional preparation and practice are expanded to encompass the current political, economic, and social realities of schooling.[32] At a time when schools are being asked to educate in the broadest sense and to accommodate children at ages younger than any of us might have thought possible ten to fifteen years ago, early childhood practitioners are in a unique and powerful position to effect the ways in which schools operate.

Notes

1 A study of educational change in which the history of the setting clearly plays a role in the change process is Louis M. Smith and P. M. Keith, *Anatomy of Educational Innovation: An Organizational Analysis of an Elementary School* (New York: John Wiley, 1971). A follow-up analysis of the above study that delineates the role of history in the Kensington innovation is Louis M. Smith et al., "Reconstructing Educational Innovation," *Teachers College Record* 80, no. 1 (Fall 1984): 20-33.

2 For a general overview see Seymour B. Sarason, *The Culture of the School and the Problem of Change*, 2nd ed. (Boston: Allyn and Bacon, 1982); and Michael Fullan, *The Meaning of Educational Change* (New York: Teachers College Press, 1982), pp. 63-73.

3 Fullan, *Meaning of Educational Change*, pp. 26-29.

4 Frances O'Connell Rust, "Implementation of an Extended Morning Kindergarten: A Case Study of an Educational Innovation" (Ed.D. diss., Teachers College, Columbia University, 1984), pp. 135-57. Also Thomas S. Popkewitz, B. Robert Tabachnick, and Gary Wehlage, *The Myth of Educational Reform* (Madison: University of Wisconsin, 1982); and Smith and Keith, *Anatomy*.

5 Rust, "Implementation of an Extended Morning Kindergarten."

6 Ibid., pp. 69-75.

7 Fullan, *Meaning of Educational Change*, pp. 54-80; and Paul Berman and Milbrey Wallin McLaughlin, *Federal Programs Supporting Educational Change, Vol. VIII, Implementing and Sustaining Innovations* (Santa Monica, Calif.: The Rand Corporation, 1978), pp. 18-21.

8 Berman and McLaughlin, *Federal Programs*, p. 16.

9 Kurt Lewin, "Group Decision and Social Change," in *Readings in Social Psychology*, ed. Edward E. MacCoby et al. (New York: Holt, Rinehart & Winston, 1958), pp. 197-211.

10 Seymour B. Sarason, *The Creation of Settings and the Future Societies* (Washington, D.C.: Jossey Bass, 1972), pp. 42-43.

11 Ibid.

12 Berman and McLaughlin, *Federal Programs*, p. 14.

13 Ibid., p. 16.

14 Ibid., pp. 14-16; and Smith and Keith, *Anatomy*.

15 Lewin, "Group Decision," pp. 197-211.

16 Berman & McLaughlin, *Federal Programs*, pp. 19-20.

17 Ibid., p. 20.

18 Fullan, *Meaning of Educational Change*, pp. 26-29.

19 Rust, "Implementation of an Extended Morning Kindergarten," pp. 134-56. See also Ernest R. House, "Three Perspectives on Innovation: Technological, Political, and Cultural," in *Improving Schools: Using What We Know*, ed. Rolf Lehming and Michael Kane (Beverly Hills: Sage Publications, 1981), pp. 17-41.

20 House, "Three Perspectives," p. 20.

21   Ibid., p. 18.

22   Ibid., p. 23.

23   Ibid., p. 25.

24   Ibid., p. 19.

25   Ibid., pp. 39–41.

26   Ibid., p. 18.

27   Ibid., p. 25.

28   Marvin Lazerson, "Historical Tensions/Future Opportunities" (Paper delivered at the invitational symposium: Defining the Field of Early Childhood Education, sponsored by the W. Alton Jones Foundation, Lincolnwood, Ill., June 2, 1988).

29   J. Victor Baldridge and Terence E. Deal, *Managing Change in Educational Institutions* (Berkeley: McCutchan Publishing, 1975), pp. 1–2. For case studies giving a general overview of educational change, see Rust, "Implementation of an Extended Morning Kindergarten"; Smith and Keith, *Anatomy*; and Harry F. Wolcott, *Teachers vs. Technocrats* (Eugene: Center for Educational Policy and Management, University of Oregon, 1977).

30   ASCD Early Childhood Education Policy Panel, "Analysis of Issues concerning Public School Involvement in Early Childhood Education," in *A Resource Guide to Public School Early Childhood Programs*, ed. Cynthia Warger (Alexandria, Va.: Association for Supervision and Curriculum Development, 1988), p. 100.

31   Berman and McLaughlin, *Federal Programs*, p. 16.

32   Jonathan G. Silin, "The Early Childhood Educator's Knowledge Base: A Reconsideration," in *Current Topics in Early Childhood Education, Vol. VII*, ed. Lilian G. Katz and Karen Steiner (Norwood, N.J.: Ablex Publishing Corporation, 1987), pp. 17–31.

The New Advocacy in Early Childhood Education

SHARON LYNN KAGAN

Yale University

How can the early childhood field receive the public support it needs? Kagan elaborates four reasons for advocacy: to preserve existing programs; to increase capacity and quality of service; to make early education more accessible, affordable, and equitable; and to educate the public about the needs of very young children and their parents in America today.

Recently a colleague, returning from a two-year stint abroad, phoned to express her amazement regarding the state of American child care and early education. A dedicated early childhood professional who lived through the birth of Head Start, the Nixon veto, and the recent lean years, Edith could not believe that thirty of the fifty governors mentioned young children in their state of the state messages, stating, "In my day, they barely knew they had children of their own!" In trying to understand why young children and families were receiving so much media and legislative attention, she queried, "Is it the work of a few sophisticated advocates or has the field become committed to public policy?" I answered by saying it was probably a little of both, and we went on to other things: her travels, our children, our work.

There can be no doubt that the early childhood profession is divided in its attitude toward the role, function, and desirability of advocacy. While some, including many practitioners, feel threatened and overwhelmed by the work of advocacy, others are invigorated by and actively engaged in advocacy activities. Reflecting on Edith's guarded interest, though, I sensed a feeling of ambivalence toward advocacy that characterizes the early childhood community. This ambivalence is particularly puzzling given that providers are passionate about creating the best environment and services for children, and given that advocacy is an effective strategy in reaching that end. Why the ambivalence? What are its sources? What are its consequences for the field of child care and early education?

WHY THE AMBIVALENCE?

This "advocacy hesitancy" did not appear spontaneously. Rather, it is rooted in the history and reality of the early childhood profession. For many years, the real practice of early childhood transpired in the classroom. Preprofessional training fortified this orientation by stressing classroom pedagogy and curricular strategies at the expense of advocacy or policy. Advocacy activities were simply considered inappropriate for professionals, especially female professionals who comprised the majority of the early childhood community. Professionalism in child care and early education stressed planting seeds in a garden with children rather than seeding ferment in statehouses or town meetings.

In the sixties, a new attitude toward social action broadly took hold: Advocacy became a successful tool for mobilizing political forces. Not only were direct advocacy efforts sanctioned, but the complementarity and potency of individual and class advocacy were recognized. Against this milieu of pervasive civil rights advocacy, the viability of child advocacy became apparent.[1] Excited by the prospects of an improved social order, many early childhood professionals became activists, focusing on the welfare of children, particularly low-income youngsters. Yet, in spite of this invigorating advocacy environment, some early childhood professionals sat back and watched as many of their colleagues burnt out in unending advocacy battles.

For those entering the field of early childhood education in the 1970s and early 1980s, a different aura prevailed. There was a pervasive sense that advocacy did not matter. Advocacy became the David pitted against a governmental Goliath, a Goliath fiercely protective of family privacy and staunchly unwilling to intervene on behalf of children and families. Advocacy values were again framed by the social context. During the 1970s and 1980s, deeply engrained cultural values exacerbated advocacy hesitancy.[2] Many felt that launching efforts in light of such tenaciously held values would be fruitless. Others feared that advocacy efforts would create a backlash that would threaten extant services. So, in just a few decades, attitudes toward advocacy shifted dramatically; however, the underlying theme of ambivalence still resounded.

In addition to attitudinal pendulum swings that provide the context for the field's advocacy history, ambivalence toward advocacy is fortified by the reality of early education. Often a moot issue, practitioner involvement in advocacy is frequently superseded by the demands of working with young children: answering children's endless questions, fetching keys out of the toilet, retrieving lost shoes, hanging paintings to dry, and so forth. Add the responsibilities of home and family to the duties of career, and it is easy to understand why many early childhood providers are precluded from advocacy work. Writing a letter to a congressman can be too much at the end of an exhausting day. Even if people are sufficiently incensed by an issue and make the time to devote to a carefully chosen cause, they still must return to their routines.[3]

Recently, however, as the early childhood field has become more policy conscious, advocacy interest has grown. Work in child and family policy and in advocacy has been accelerated by the timely collision of research, demographics, corporate concern, and growing media attention to child and family issues. Realizing that the time is ripe, increasing numbers of advocates have begun to mobilize. New advocacy groups have been formed, such as the Child Care Action Campaign; older and more established groups, for example, Child Care, Inc., have garnered foundation support to carry out their work; and coalitions of advocates have joined forces to support legislation.

One successful coalition, the Pre-kindergarten Alliance, came together to support passage and monitor implementation of the New York City early childhood initiative, Project Giant Step. This alliance was "almost unprecedented in city history"[4] and was instrumental in bringing the program to reality. Recent activities of the New York City–based Center for Public Advocacy Research fortified this commitment to collaboration. In concert with other statewide advocacy organizations, the center (through its Omnibus Child Care Act activities) worked to draft state legislation that would establish the Office of Child Day Care Services.[5]

Nationwide, early childhood professionals are counseling the field on the rationale for and strategies in advocacy.[6] National advocacy groups are encouraging the development of statewide groups. In sum, advocacy in early childhood, despite a rocky road, is coming into its own.

PROBLEMS IN ADVOCACY

In spite of current interest in advocacy among the early childhood community, several gnawing issues must be addressed if the field is to capitalize on this current surge of pro-advocacy sentiment. First, the early childhood profession needs to understand who the advocates are and to discern appropriate and synergistic roles for those involved. Advocacy organizations, though burgeoning, are staffed for the most part by people not working directly with children and families. The field applauds the many "professional advocates" who do possess field experience; however, many of them lack this background. Their visions of advocacy emerge from textbooks rather than from experience. While not necessarily negative, this perspective slants the substance of advocacy work undertaken and alters expectations of what practitioners could and should do. Lofty expectations present the potential for strong conflict between professional advocates and practitioners despite their frequent unity of vision.

Second, although coalitions are crucial in strengthening the influence of advocacy efforts in the political arena,[7] and although significant efforts at coalition building have been made, obstacles to forming successful coalitions persist. Clearly the most basic is that, since individuals and organizations have their own priorities, ideas, beliefs, and agendas (and, in fact, the advancement of an organization's interests may be one of the main reasons for joining a coalition[8]), it is often difficult for various organizations to agree on mutually acceptable positions. Agreement is particularly difficult when the issue is complex, as is often the case with early childhood concerns. Additionally, the likelihood of interest-group conflict is maximized when the period between the emergence of an issue and the time when final action is necessary is short.[9] This, too, is often the case in child care and early education. Further, successful coalition building is hampered by the absence of coalition experience in the human service field generally[10] and in early education specifically. Because early childhood professionals are represented by disparate interest groups spanning various sectors, and because these professionals are comparatively inexperienced in coalition building, the task is large.

Third, and very important, while many practitioners believe advocacy is important, it is still perceived as tangential to their immediate work. For example, when given choices at professional conferences between sessions on advocacy and curriculum-related workshops, practitioners consistently prefer the latter. To explain practitioners' less than wild enthusiasm for advocacy, professional advocates conjecture that practitioners are intimidated by advocacy and frightened by their own ignorance of advocacy procedures.[11] Westman suggests that people are paralyzed by their uncertainty of what to do.[12] They fear causing more harm than good and so remain inactive. Fishhaut offers successful strategies to ease practitioner involvement into the advocacy arena.[13] In order to help minimize this "how to" insecurity, the role of advocacy in preservice training should be legitimized, with concrete proactive strategies taught. In a review of numerous child advocacy training efforts, Cahill found an absence of a rational, structured approach.[14] Responding to this deficit, he developed a training curriculum grounded in both the history and the process of advocacy.

While the absence of specific how-to training may explain practitioners' advocacy hesitancy in part, we cannot attribute this ambivalence to lack of training alone. Such an analysis ignores the phenomenology of the history and culture of early childhood care and education. When that is considered, it becomes clear that what is missing is not simply lessons on *how* to advocate, but the motivation for action that comes from knowing *why* advocacy is critical. What is the rationale for advocacy and why is it the lifeline of early childhood education?

WHY ADVOCATE?

Advocacy in the child care and early education field has four main rationales, all of which are critically important to practitioners: (1) to preserve programs and safeguard slots for youngsters; (2) to increase service capacity, to enhance program quality, or to demonstrate that a new idea or program type can work, as in funding for demonstration programs; (3) to change the systemic infrastructure of the field, thereby making child care and early education more accessible, affordable, and equitable; and (4) to generate public awareness of the issues facing the field and facing children and parents.

The major advocacy efforts of the early and mid-1980s focused primarily on the first category, preserving and safeguarding services occasioned by budget cuts. More recent initiatives differ dramatically in both number and intent from efforts of the past and represent the second category, increasing services. For example, since 1980, twenty-one states have passed legislation and/or appropriated state revenues for state pre-kindergarten programs, and since 1984, five have initiated contributions to Head Start to expand and/or improve services. Additional states have established task forces and commissions to address categories three and four, revamping the infrastructure and increasing public awareness.[15] These new forums for early childhood concerns offer ready opportunities for advocacy. Additionally, the existence of these arenas and the climate preceding their creation practically require that action be taken lest these opportunities pass.

At the federal level, 107 child- and family-related bills are being considered, including the landmark Act for Better Child Care, Senator Orrin Hatch's Child Care Improvement Act, Senator Christopher Dodd's New School Childcare Demonstration Projects Act of 1987, and Senator Edward Kennedy's Smart Start. Because the philosophies on which these are based and the ultimate goals they are designed to accomplish vary, the bills differ on nearly all but the most global goal of expanding services, the second advocacy rationale. How they propose to do this differs dramatically. Some attach programs to existing services (Head Start or child care); some implement demonstration projects; and some expand via the public schools. While some bills speak to enhancing quality, others remain silent, hoping states will act on regulatory issues. Attempting to make child care more accessible, affordable, and equitable, the third advocacy rationale, some bills help all families; others, in contrast, focus on low- and middle-income families. The proposed legislation varies on nearly all dimensions. Some bills are age restricted; some are not. Some provide resource and referral services; some do not. Some consider family day care; some focus exclusively on center care. Precisely because of their abundance and variation, these bills require a level of study, analysis, and advocacy work unparalleled in the field's history.

ADVOCACY IN ACTION

Given the urgent need for advocacy for young children and their families, just how does one go about this? Theorists suggest that the appropriateness of method depends on the issue, the forum, and the individuals involved.[16] Several strategies warrant particular attention. Critical analytic attention must be accorded the Alliance for Better Child Care (ABC) as the most dramatic example of advocacy collaboration. At the national level, ABC will teach the field important lessons about how a children's agenda can be advanced. To be effective, however, advocacy must also be rooted at the state and community levels. Pelosi proposes a model community-based advocacy system that utilizes existing organizations and specifies relationships between the system's components, and between the system and the community.[17] Adaptive to meet a community's changing needs, modifiable depending on neighborhood resources, and capable of individual and class advocacy, this model includes: (1) monitoring and assessing to identify advocacy needs; (2) management to set goals and distribute resources; and (3) action to design alternative projects or interventions and to obtain resources and implement designated plans. Perlman offers another alternative delineating three types of grass-roots groups: those that use direct action to pressure existing institutions to be more accountable, those that use the electoral system to replace existing institutions, and those that form alternative institutions to bypass existing powers.[18] While complementary, these approaches may even be most successful when combined in an advocacy initiative, according to Perlman.

Building on Pelosi's list of advocacy functions, others cite educating the community and political decision makers through speaking engagements and the media, developing proposals based on the consensus of a majority of the organizations participating in the advocacy effort, forming additional and more representative alliances, and working in the court system.[19]

In addition to advocacy at the community, state, and national levels, there is an educative component to advocacy. Advocacy not only involves political mobilization on behalf of specific programs and services, but embraces the generation and dissemination of knowledge. Educating parents regarding quality and the issues affecting quality is one form of public education, the fourth reason to advocate. Providing information and support to parents so that they can be effective advocates for their children and their children's programs is a linchpin of quality early education. Goffin even suggests that personal advocacy be part of each practitioner's job description, and that the parent-provider relationship be actively, extensively, and intentionally viewed as a forum for advocacy.[20]

CONDITIONS FOR ADVOCACY IN EARLY CHILDHOOD

Given the particular history that pervades advocacy in child care and early childhood education, I suggest that four conditions are necessary before the field orchestrates large-scale efforts. *First, all early childhood professionals must stop regarding advocacy as aberrant leftist behavior and start treasuring it as a national resource.* Advocacy is the fuel that drives programs; without it, programs cease to exist. To ensure robust advocacy efforts, the nation must make advocacy an enduring part of its social system.[21] Specifically, incoming professionals must be socialized to roles not only as future educators and caregivers, but as future advocates. To legitimate advocacy, practitioners need to understand the importance of the advocacy process and their critical role in it. Given their understanding of children and families, they are particularly well situated to be effective advocates.[22] By understanding the legislative process and policy implications, they can increase their potency.

Second, advocacy must be greased. In Congress, when the term *greased* is used it means the wheels have been well oiled, the planning has been carefully done, and action is ready to begin. Advocates need to be well greased not just on strategy, but on substance.[23] Their work must be thorough and not based on superficial assumptions about children.[24] All too often, advocates reduce their own potency because they see reality through one side of a prism. Only when advocates are scrupulously objective in gathering and using data will they be regarded with credibility by policymakers. Being well prepared also means building constituencies across traditional interest groups and across professional disciplines.[25] Unfortunately, advocacy organizations all too often lose their potency by falling prey to exactly the same syndrome they charge bureaucracies with: turf guarding. Weisner describes situations in which legislators are bombarded with a disorganized collection of special interests as the "competitive model" of coalitions.[26] He explains that this approach is generally poorly received and will not benefit these interests. No matter how well greased the wheels, if advocacy organizations are fractured they cannot go far.

Third, the advocacy community must work with early childhood practitioners to carve out realistic, appropriate, and differentiated roles for advocates and practitioners. Professional advocates need to spend time courting practitioners, not only policymakers. It is exciting and chic to solicit support in state capitols and Washington, D.C., but this must not be done at the expense of soliciting support in local neighborhoods and communities. Practitioners offer perspectives and connections that will aid advocacy efforts. In return, professional advocates must assist practitioners in understanding the consequences of various policy initiatives in terms of their own programs. How would the addition of a school-based initiative impact my program? Which pieces of legislation would enable my community to augment its services most appropriately? Whether such analyses are done on a program basis or in concert with other community providers, the first lens must focus on impact at the program and local level.[27]

The fourth condition is that advocates must ground their positions in principles of child development. By doing so, advocates will automatically be required to place priority on quality and continuity in children's services. A "more slots" approach to policy is not sufficient. The field must craft a long-haul vision that simultaneously increases services and addresses the following problems, which are endemic to the field: (1), compensation and benefits; (2) the dichotomy between care and education; and (3) the social stratification of children.

Clearly, the issue of insufficient compensation, including working conditions and benefits, must be addressed if the profession is to advance. The difficulty of attracting early childhood staff will foster "staff-stealing" and continue to pit programs against each other. An overall strategy, devised to attract and recruit qualified people into child care and early education and to pay them adequately, is a necessary precondition for program expansion. No matter how many slots are funded, unless there are enough providers to teach children in these slots, programs will be precluded from opening. Stated simply, program expansion will be capped without adequate personnel. Program quality will also be diminished because, without adequate compensation, caregivers will leave the field, causing discontinuity for children and programs.

While the field is acknowledging that the dichotomy between care and education is a rhetorical rather than a reality-based issue, proposed legislation, with only a few exceptions, perpetuates the care-versus-education debate. As individuals and as a field, the early childhood community must stem the public perception that care is not educational and that education is not caring. The field must encourage people to acknowledge that quality exists in all sectors. All early childhood professionals need to guard against legislation that will fragment the field and work to ensure collaboration across sectors and programs. The field must stop stressing differences between care and education, and realize that legislative and programmatic success are contingent on a common vision.

Finally, for decades federal and state child care and early education policies have perpetuated intense social and economic stratification of children. Many programs have been established with stringent guidelines, making them accessible only to special-needs or low-income youngsters. Middle- and higher-income families must seek programs elsewhere. In effect, early childhood policies segregate preschool-age children by income when integration is the law for school-age youngsters who are merely one year older. While on the brink of exciting new efforts on behalf of children, the field of early childhood care and education must look beyond "more slots" and use these opportunities to alter policy stances that stratify children.

This is a new era, an era in which each member of the early childhood community has the chance to redress inequities in the field that have been troubling for so long. Now there is the chance to make some fundamental improvements that will improve child care and early education in this country for years to come. We must put ambivalence aside, muster our energy, and stay informed and active. The profession needs all its members, practitioners and advocates, now as never before.

Notes

1   Jack C. Westman, *Child Advocacy: New Professional Roles for Helping Families* (New York: The Free Press, 1979), p. xiv.

2   Brian F. Cahill, "Training Volunteers as Child Advocates," *Child Welfare* 7, no. 6 (November–December 1986): 548.

3   Janice E. Perlman, "Grassrooting the System," *Social Policy* 7 (September–October 1976): 6.

4   Toni Porter, "New Alliance Urges $39 Million for Education for Four Year Olds" (Report prepared for Child Care, Inc., May 1986), p. 3.

5   Caroline Zinsser, "Current Activities in Child Care and Early Childhood Education Advocacy and Research" (Memo prepared for the Center for Public Advocacy Research, New York, June 1988).

6   Erna Fishhaut, "A Time to Dream: A Call for Action," *Young Children*, November 1987, pp. 20–22; and Stacie G. Goffin, "Putting Our Advocacy Efforts into a New Context," *Young Children*, March 1988, pp. 52–56.

7   Maria Roberts-DeGennaro, "Building Coalitions for Political Advocacy," *Social Work* 31 (July-August 1986): 308.

8   Stan Weisner, "Fighting Back: A Critical Analysis of Coalition Building in the Human Services," *Social Service Review* 57 (June 1983): 296.

9   Roberts-DeGennaro, "Building Coalitions," p. 309.

10   Weisner, "Fighting Back," p. 296.

11   Cahill, "Training Volunteers," pp. 545–53; and Roberts-DeGennaro, "Building Coalitions," p. 308.

12   Westman, *Child Advocacy*, p. xiv.

13   Fishhaut, "A Time to Dream," pp. 20–22.

14   Cahill, "Training Volunteers," p. 546.

15   Fern Marx, "Current Early Childhood Initiatives in the States" (Report prepared for The Early Childhood Development Task Force, Connecticut Commission on Children, November 1987), p. 1.

16   Fishhaut, "A Time to Dream," p. 22.

17   John W. Pelosi, "Advocacy System: Generic Components," in *Child Advocacy within the System*, ed. J. L. Paul, G. R. Neufeld, and J. W. Pelosi (Syracuse, N.Y.: Syracuse University Press, 1977), pp. 32–40.

18   Perlman, "Grassrooting the System," p. 8.

19   Fishhaut, "A Time to Dream," p. 22; and Roberts-DeGennaro, "Building Coalitions," p. 310.

20   Goffin, "Putting Our Advocacy Efforts into a New Context," p. 52.

21   Westman, *Child Advocacy*, p. 45.

22   Fishhaut, "A Time to Dream," p. 22; and Roberts-DeGennaro, "Building Coalitions," p. 308.

23   Cahill, "Training Volunteers," p. 545.

24   Westman, *Child Advocacy*, p. 50.

25   Fishhaut, "A Time to Dream," p. 22; Weisner, "Fighting Back," p. 293; and Westman, *Child Advocacy*, pp. 50–51.

26   Weisner, "Fighting Back," p. 293.

27   Cahill, "Training Volunteers," p. 550; and Pelosi, "Advocacy System," p. 32.

New Visions, New Voices:
Future Directions in the Care and
Education of Young Children

LESLIE R. WILLIAMS
Teachers College, Columbia University

In both summing up and looking ahead, Williams sets the parameters for answering four basic questions: Who should be served? What should be our goals? How best can we deliver needed services? And how should we prepare early childhood specialists?

Every generation is concerned with the care and education of the young, and every generation of caregivers and educators has its visionaries. This generation is no exception. Poised at the beginning of a decade marking the end of one century and the beginning of a new one, commentators on the field of early childhood are finding that looking ahead has a special appeal. New times often bring fresh perspectives on enduring dilemmas, as well as a renewed sense of urgency to their consideration. At this moment, early childhood specialists are in a unique position to bring synthesis to the evolution of the field and to consider the dynamics of human growth and development, with an eye to the implications of such study for the future of early childhood in particular and for society in general.

Articles in professional journals focusing on the early childhood years now frequently note that public and private involvement with the well-being, nurturance, and education of young children is currently assuming unprecedented proportions in the United States. Much of today's professional engagement in early childhood concerns has arisen from distinctive histories, as a function of widely varying perceptions of the needs of the populations to be served.[1] Other involvements seem to have come from acceptance of particular theoretical premises, or from the inheritance of more than two centuries of practice.[2] In juxtaposition to these internal realities are the external inducements of changing demographics in our population's increasing cultural diversity, in a shifting composition of the work force with concomitant redefinition of the family, in rising numbers of young children in schools and caregiving arrangements outside of the home, and in increasingly severe teacher/caregiver shortages.[3]

The multidimensionality of the current activity in early childhood education and child care can give the impression of fragmentation of the field. It is not always easy to detect the emerging inner coherence that is leading to finer resolution of the issues underlying the field's rapid expansion. Much can be learned, however, from listening carefully to those who describe the multiple involvements of early childhood researchers, practitioners, and policymakers.

The authors of this special issue of the *Record* represent a sample of these voices, and their collected articles reveal some of the field's inner structures. Particularly telling are the debates around four classic concerns in the broader field of education applied to early childhood, namely, (1) identification and characterization of the populations to be served, (2) definition of the goals of the services to be provided, (3) delineation of optimal settings for delivery of service, and (4) preparation of the persons responsible for the study, nurturance, and education of young children.[4] These considerations suggest emerging future directions of the field, as they underscore the potential for positively influencing children's lives.

POPULATIONS TO BE SERVED

Identification of the populations to be addressed in the work currently revolves around the existence of limited resources. In light of the relatively low national priority given to the care and education of our children (in comparison with other items on the federal budget[5]), and a growing scarcity of early childhood practitioners, what characteristics should guide our decisions for intervention?

Moynihan and Edelman argue that disenfranchisement of large numbers of young children is occurring through both political and economic structures in our society. It is the children of the poor, the children whose primary caregivers are working or are otherwise unavailable to them for a large portion of each day, who are most in need of a high quality of service. Both authors indicate the barriers in existing legislation to access to early childhood programs. Both also point out the likely deleterious effects of lack of access on struggling families and on the development of individual children within them.

Schorr highlights another dimension to this concern by showing that the children for whom positive effects of early intervention have most clearly been demonstrated are those most likely to be at risk — the same children whose families have limited economic means, and who frequently have problems associated with poverty, such as unwanted pregnancies, inadequate or abusive parenting, family discord, or residence in troubled neighborhoods.

Comer's examination of the effects of racism on the growth and development of young children and Moynihan's demonstration of the influence of racism on policymaking add another dimension to the issue of intervention. In the United States one's chances of being at risk are greatly increased by being a child of color. Not only is access to services limited, but individuals who are within existing programs in schools are likely to experience negative reactions to their presence that have damaging effects on their sense of self, their efficacy, and their aspirations.

The implication of these arguments is that the populations to be addressed most immediately are those in danger of being lost to our society, the children whose families cannot yet derive full advantage from the economic, political, social, and educational systems of our country. This approach accepts (even though it does not agree with) the reality of limited budgetary allocations and seeks the most effective possible use of existing resources.

In counterpoint to acceptance of the position of trying to do more with less is a drive by other advocates toward expanding the resource pool. In her presentation of child care and early childhood education as a unified service model, Caldwell looks toward redefinition of the scope and province of public education. In her vision, public schools should not only expand the age span of the children they serve but the hours of service, making available to all children a high quality of care and education.

Such an approach implies fundamental changes in the existing structure of public schools, changes that would require, among other elements, increasing sensitivity to diversity of characteristics in the children and families served. Rust's examination of the dynamics of change reminds us again of the profound influence of sociocultural context (e.g., sets of beliefs and expectations within a community, existing educational practices, issues of power and control in resource allocation, and the professional images of early childhood educators and caregivers) in the consideration of such a reorientation of priorities.

There is another reason why reorientation of public priorities toward increased support of early education and child care may be important. That reason concerns what we are beginning to discover about the nature of the young child as a learner. Lee's reassessment of the literature on perspective-taking in young children strongly suggests that even the very young construct knowledge of the world through perceptions of the social and physical contexts in which new information appears. By extension, we can speculate that from infancy onward, children are peculiarly sensitive to the subtle messages conveyed in social exchange, and, even more than we previously surmised, are likely to be negatively affected by such configurations as inconsistent care, disrupted attachment bonds, racial discrimination, or developmentally inappropriate teaching methods. Lack of attention to the needs of young children and their families now, in this time of rapid social change, may have serious repercussions in the future.

If, indeed, children's psyches are so permeable to social and societal constructs, then the issue of increasing cultural diversity in the populations served in child care and early childhood education settings also assumes greater significance. Difference in children's opportunities due to their socioeconomic status has already been pointed out. The negative effects that may result from uninformed response to conflicts between the home culture and the culture of the school or center (for example, in expectations for the child's behavior, ways of acquiring knowledge, or modes for expression of approval) have begun to be explored only relatively recently.[6] Differences resulting from culture are still frequently confused with those occasioned by socioeconomic class, leading to the assumption that their resolution is entirely economic or political in nature. Yet many cultural differences (such as observance of particular religious practices, languages spoken, or aesthetic ideals) may cut across social class and must be addressed through other means. Moreover, we now know that difference does not necessarily mean deficit, and that effective interventions can result from leading from strength.[7] Reexamination of educational goals, design of culturally sensitive settings for early learning, and preparation of caregivers and teachers to utilize cultural differences constructively in the teaching and learning processes are all possibilities for future interconnections between home and school.

Still another aspect of the issue of the populations to be served is definition of the needs and capabilities of infants and consequently, of the nature of their inclusion in the study, research, and practice of early childhood. The fact that in this collection of articles, only two authors specifically mention infants, and then only briefly, suggests that infant study and practice remains a specialization within the field. Originating from a combination of studies in psychology and clinical practice, work in the area of infancy has tended to focus on either support of children and families at risk due to problems of substance abuse, deprivation, or stressful life-style, or on the reinforcement of early learning through parenting skills and attitudes.[8] Still, increasing numbers of infants are now in group-care arrangements, and the work of Brazelton, Stern, Provence, Axtmann, and others, indicate that even very young children are able to benefit from intentionally prepared settings that foster interpersonal interactions with peers and adults, as well as engagement with a rich physical environment.[9] It is probable that future development in the field will see a greater integration of the concerns of infant study and practice.

GOALS OF THE SERVICES TO BE PROVIDED

The issue of goals is closely tied to definition of the populations to be served. The determination of the content of child care and early education programs has inspired one of the longest debates in the field. Caldwell notes that the original schism between child care and early childhood education arose from the conception of different purposes for different populations. Children from families whose financial resources were limited were understood to need custodial programs to safeguard their welfare while their parents were at work. On the other hand, children from more affluent families (where, it was assumed, one parent remained at home) were seen as benefiting from educationally oriented programs, usually of only a half day's duration. Schisms of this sort, historically not uncommon in the field of early childhood,[10] expressed a deeper tension between opposing views on the nature of the field's study and practice. The controversy might be better understood if it is seen as moving back and forth across two intersecting axes, between values and science[11] and the individual and society,[12] as shown in Figure 1.

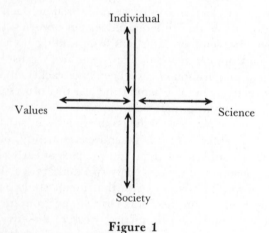

Figure 1

The first fifty years of early childhood theory and practice were dominated by the Froebelian kindergarten, an educational program expressive of a highly elaborated value system. The work was inspired by a particular vision of the human spirit, and aimed at the reformation of society through inculcation of moral as well as intellectual training at an early age. By the turn of the century, the Progressive movement had achieved sufficient momentum to challenge the Froebelian kindergarten in the name of science. The rising tide of child study, and the derivation of early childhood practice from observation of individual children's capacities and needs, eventually moved the field of early childhood away from consideration of underlying value systems.[13] Developmental descriptions, psychodynamic perspectives, and behavorial theory each in turn became the dominant force influencing study and practice. These varying points of departure produced characterizations of the nature of the young child that had distinctive implications for practice.

The common thread in resulting programs (in spite of the wide variety of their expression) was that they were all seen as representative of science.[14]

This movement reached its apogee from the early 1960s to the mid-1970s, when federal funding was available for the expansion of early childhood programs. A key feature of this funding, however, was that it was targeted toward a very specific population, the children of poverty. Much energy, therefore, went into identification of the needs of that group, viewed monolithically. The characterization of poor children as deficient in the skills and attitudes required for success in the existing school system led directly to the design of programs focused on rapid acquisition of those skills and attitudes. The goal of those programs was remediation of "disadvantagement."[15]

In contrast to this emphasis was the curriculum development undertaken for more affluent segments of our society during the same period. There, the emphasis was on enrichment and extension of the children's existing capabilities to sharpen our competitive edge in scientific and technological pursuits.[16] Disenfranchisement and the question of what sort of education was to be available to whom reintroduced the question of values into early childhood study and practice, and shifted focus in some cases back from the needs of the individual to the good of society. Throughout the 1980s, the interplay between science and values and between the individual and society has continued its fascinating dynamic, shaping debate even as it moves the field toward increasing internal coherence.

The energy of the continuing discussion and the emerging synthesis of previously dichotomous positions are revealed clearly in the collected articles of this issue of the *Record*. Schorr, Lee, Haskins and Alessi, Caldwell, and Rust speak in their various ways to science, while not ignoring the sociocultural influences that are ultimately rooted in perception of value. Moynihan, Edelman, Comer, Fromberg, Magid, Bowman, and Kagan address issues of what effort is worthwhile in early childhood education and child care (a question of values), while acknowledging the importance of articulated knowledge bases for grounding study and practice. Moynihan, Edelman, Caldwell, Haskins and Alessi, Magid, and Rust wed values and science to a view of what is good for society as a whole; while Comer, Schorr, Lee, Fromberg, and Bowman are essentially concerned with the study and effects of practice on the development of individual children (though they clearly recognize the impact of social interaction on individual development).

Another aspect of the discussion around goals for study, research, and service in the field is that of appropriate content for early childhood programs. Much of the original concern about serving populations characterized as disadvantaged centered on discovering ways to change children (by inculcating repertoires of skills and attitudes related to later school success) to meet the existing expectations and structures of formal education. More recently, early childhood specialists have spoken persuasively to the converse of that position. They are looking for ways to change the schools and other early childhood settings to support the knowledge and skills children bring with them to the learning situation, reflect specific learning characteristics, and address the needs of their families.[17]

From that perspective, teachers/caregivers must assume more of a mediational role than a shaping or transmitting one. Through their observation of children at work and play, they derive the particulars of their practice, offering the learning materials and activities that are most likely to motivate children and encourage increasingly higher levels of accomplishment.

This orientation has revitalized consideration of the "whole child" as the subject of study, research, and practice in the field. Representing a motif that has distinguished early childhood from elementary school practice during most of the field's history, this view of the indivisibility of a child's developmental needs, capabilities, and interests has clear implications for program content. Rather than short-term goals (achievement in subject areas alone, or isolated acquisition of formal skills), long-term goals (such as the development of social and emotional coping capacities, creative and critical thinking skills, and refined psychomotoric capabilities) define the content of the programs. The activities offered young children are designed to integrate subject areas, reflect children's ongoing experience, and require the children's direct engagement with the physical and social environments in which they are working. Paper-and-pencil tasks are introduced as natural outcomes of experimentation with objects, rather than as major vehicles for concept acquisition. Experiential rather than verbal verification is sought through individual and small-group activity around malleable and manipulative materials. Language is developed and extended in conjunction with such activity, rather than as a goal in itself.[18]

The implications drawn by Schorr, Fromberg, Caldwell, Haskins and Alessi, and Bowman represent these dispositions in several ways. Schorr's citing the characteristics of successful interventions highlights the importance of focus on underlying processes rather than on products as avenues to changing outcomes for children. Haskins and Alessi's developmental model for early childhood centers embodies those characteristics, as Fromberg's intellectual/experiential paradigm and Caldwell's comprehensive model. Bowman's view of the appropriateness of integration of the subjective and reflective with the objective dimensions of knowledge reaffirms the role of experience in extending our capabilities as learners and as teachers. Transformation and evolution of socioemotional, cognitive, and psychomotor capacities become the goals of early childhood programs, rather than the reproduction of existing structures of knowledge.

OPTIMAL SETTINGS FOR DELIVERY OF SERVICE

With such a vision of the appropriate content for early childhood programs comes reconsideration of the settings conducive to its attainment. If form is to follow function, the structures of services offered must be reshaped to be expressive of the stated intents. The collected articles in this special issue of the *Record* point strongly to the likelihood that change must occur on several levels simultaneously—the levels of national policy, local practice, and individual commitment.

Moynihan, Edelman, and Magid point out that both political and economic concerns dictate significant extension of the supports provided young children and their families, if we are not to lose a large proportion of our human resources in the coming years. Explicit recognition of the connections between nurturance of young children and their families and expansion of an increasingly capable national work force must result in stronger public and private engagement with child care and early childhood education. In short, the money must be found, and legislation backing the allocation of funds must be passed.

In regard to local practice, current discussion of optimal settings for delivery of services brings two thoughts immediately to mind. First, in contrast to consideration of the design of settings a decade ago, the emphasis now is on the intimate connection between the care and education of young children and broader societal patterns. Meeting the need for familial support through reconceptualization of the uses of space and time brings new parameters to the meaning of nurturance of the whole child.

Caldwell, for example, offers a template for restructuring public schools to reflect the learning styles and developmental needs of young children, while also responding to emerging societal needs. The articulation of programs for children from infancy through the elementary years speaks to the creation of a connection and continuity in children's care and educational experience that might not otherwise be available in a society undergoing such rapid change. Magid suggests that employer-supported child care may have returns not only in increase in overall productivity for the parents, but in the stress relief for adults that may well enhance the well-being of their children.

At the same time, though, reflection in program design of changing societal structures may bring with it an inherent danger. Thoughtless reproduction of societal patterns may foster disregard for the learning characteristics and the physical and psychological needs of young children. Fromberg comments on the move to full- or extended-day kindergartens in the public schools with a cautionary note on loss of vision in the process. Expanded settings must reflect expanded goals. Rust urges that our professional consciousness be raised in regard to the dynamics of change so that we might avoid such a subversion of our purpose.

Local practice should be guided by what we are now beginning to know about the contexts of effective teaching, and young children's development and learning. This rubric implies that networks for the exchange of information and insight must be refined and extended to encompass all regions of the country and of the world where innovation in practice is yielding outstanding results.[19] Part of that linkage ought to bolster ongoing consideration of what constitutes quality in the delivery of service, and of the relationship between quality and the design of settings. Some of the excellent work already done in that area needs to be made more widely available, cutting across lines still drawn by program sponsorship.[20]

Attention to issues of quality, however, requires not only access to the most current information, but also individual commitment on the part of persons responsible for program implementation. Kagan offers a vision of the concerned person as enactor, as a person who can change unacceptable circumstances through informed and concerted action. Advocacy must become a stronger part of the professional repertoire of all those who create settings for the care and education of young children.

PREPARATION OF EARLY CHILDHOOD SPECIALISTS

Professional repertoires will be only as good as the programs of preparation that engender them. If we expect to have a cadre of knowledgeable, reflective individuals who will guide and promote change with the best interests of children in mind, we must attend to the quality of teacher/caregiver preparation and to the licensure that follows.

Awareness of children's extraordinary sensitivity to social contexts in their construction of knowledge (Lee), reflection on the quality and outcomes of one's own experience as a child (Bowman), and recognition of unconscious absorption of societal structures such as racism (Comer) must be addressed explicitly in programs of preparation as avenues to refinement of practice. These parameters may mean a total reexamination of the assumptions early childhood teacher educators have made regarding what are important skills and knowledge for novice practitioners.

For more experienced practitioners as well as novices, there are strong implications for refinement of their work in reassessment of the early childhood teacher/caregiver's role as one of mediator. In the discussion above of appropriate content for early childhood programs, the image of mediator appeared a more accurate representation of actual functions than those of transmitter of knowledge or shaper of behavior. Rust and her colleagues have previously suggested that the familiar curriculum triangle of child, teacher, and content should be reconceptualized to a three-dimensional figure, with child, community (including parents), and administration at the three corners, and the teacher in the center negotiating content with the other three parties.[21] I would extend that image further by saying that more than ever, early childhood specialists are becoming mediators between children and the increasingly complex sociocultural contexts of their lives, between parents and the school, between themselves and their colleagues, and between their own inner perceptions of what should be and what is. They are seeking guidance about how to proceed in this complicated negotiation, and it should be the responsibility of programs of preparation to provide such guidance.

Reconsideration of the content of programs of preparation begs a parallel focus on teacher/caregiver certification and licensure. Fromberg argues that the lack of explicit recognition of the specialized nature of the preparation of early childhood staff endemic in many state certification procedures must be remediated. If, as has been suggested above, programs of preparation incorporate new dimensions, then certification must take those dimensions into account. At a point in time when many states are resisting or giving only minimal attention to recognition of a specialization in early childhood, such a focus will require concentrated advocacy on the part of professional organizations to accomplish its end.

CONCLUSION

The current multiplicity of early childhood concerns can be partly understood by extracting themes from a representative collection of articles, as has been done above. A deeper level of understanding may come, however, by looking again at the breadth of the undertakings and by the search for appropriate language to voice concerns.

The articles in this issue underscore the fact that there is currently a rapid expansion in the vision of the possible in the field of early childhood, and a concomitant intersection of the concerns of young children with almost every dimension of society. Political, economic, educational, and social institutions are all profoundly affected by and have an impact on the nurturance of young children. What once in our history was considered essentially a private concern is increasingly becoming a public charge.

The communication of that charge in language that is publicly accessible and genuinely descriptive is becoming, therefore, more and more urgent. Early childhood specialists cannot allow their professional conversations to exclude those whose understanding and support of their undertakings will be critical to their success. A vocabulary and a style of communication must be developed that is both straightforward and powerful, avoiding jargon, yet encouraging precision in identification and discussion of our concerns.

As in any developing field, problems in precision of language stem from several sources. One difficulty in past work has come from over-reliance on the vocabulary of psychology — a tendency that has led to an emphasis on individual development without consistent reference to the social contexts in which that development occurs. More recent movement toward incorporation of anthropological and sociological constructs into early childhood analyses has brought the opposite difficulty — loss of focus on the individual's distinctive characteristics in favor of the group.

In a similar fashion, early childhood specialists and commentators have not always taken into account the value systems expressed in their discourse. Sometimes relying on anecdotal evidence alone for their claims, they have not always examined the lenses through which they have seen the incidents reported. In the interest of science, however, much of the richness of what actually occurred in a program, a classroom, or with individual children has also been lost.

This circumstance suggests that an important activity of the field will continue to be refinement of the expression of its distinctive perspectives, and articulation of those perspectives with those emerging in allied fields. Such refinement will be the clarifying medium for tomorrow's visions.

Notes

1 Bernard Spodek, Olivia N. Saracho, and Donald L. Peters, "Professionalism, Semiprofessionalism, and Craftsmanship," in *Professionalism and the Early Childhood Practitioner*, ed. Bernard Spodek, Olivia N. Saracho, and Donald L. Peters (New York: Teachers College Press, 1988), pp. 3–6.

2 Jonathan G. Silin, "The Early Childhood Educator's Knowledge Base: A Reconsideration," in *Current Topics in Early Childhood Education*, vol. 7, ed. Lilian G. Katz (Norwood, N.J.: Ablex Publishing Corporation, 1987), pp. 17–18; and Ruby Takanishi, "Early Childhood Education and Research: The Changing Relationship," *Theory into Practice* 20 (1981): 86–93.

3 Dana Friedman, *Encouraging Employer Supports to Working Parents: Community Strategies for Change* (New York: The Carnegie Corporation, 1983); and *A Nation Prepared: Teachers for the 21st Century*, Report of the Task Force on Teaching as a Profession (New York: Carnegie Forum on Education and the Economy, 1986), pp. 26–32.

4 These questions were derived from those posed by Samuel J. Braun and Esther P. Edwards in *History and Theory of Early Childhood Education* (Worthington, Ohio: Charles A. Jones Publishing, 1972), pp. 8–9.

5 *Children's Defense Budget, FY 1989* (Washington, D.C.: Children's Defense Fund, 1988), pp. 1–4.

6 Patricia G. Ramsey, Edwina B. Vold, and Leslie R. Williams, *A Source Book on Multicultural Education* (New York: Garland Publishing, 1989), pp. 43–78, 87–88, 163–64.

7 A number of unpublished reports of federally funded educational projects have yielded this finding. An example is Herminio Martinez et al., "Evaluation Report of the Cross-Cultural Demonstration Project" (Final report; New York: Institute of Urban and Minority Education, 1985).

8 For a sampling of the topics currently being discussed in the area of infancy, see *Zero to Three*, published periodically by The National Center for Clinical Infant Programs, Washington, D.C.

9 T. Berry Brazelton, "New Knowledge about the Infant from Current Research: Implications for Psychoanalysis" (Paper presented at the American Psychoanalytic Association Meeting, San Francisco, California, May 1980); Daniel N. Stern, *The Interpersonal World of the Infant: A View from Psychoanalysis and Developmental Psychology* (New York: Basic Books, 1985); Sally Provence, Audrey Naylor, and June Patterson, *The Challenge of Day Care* (New Haven: Yale University Press, 1977); and Annette Axtmann, "A Setting for Study and Support," *Zero to Three* 20, no. 3 (February 1984): 4–8.

10   Other examples would be the preparation of caregivers versus the preparation of teachers in particular university settings, the discontinuity between infancy studies and the general field of early childhood, and the theoretical orientation of nursery schools versus that of many kindergartens.

11   The rooting of early childhood practice in values as well as science has been discussed by Bernard Spodek in "What Are the Sources of Early Childhood Curriculum?" *Young Children* 26, no. 1 (January 1970): 48–59; Millie Almy, "The Early Childhood Educator Revisited," in *Professionalism and the Early Childhood Practitioner*, ed. Spodek, Saracho, and Peters, pp. 48–55; and Leslie R. Williams, "Determining the Curriculum," in *The Early Childhood Curriculum: A Review of Current Research*, ed. Carol Seefeldt (New York: Teachers College Press, 1987), pp. 1–12.

12   The juxtaposition of the individual and society as an aim of education was frequently discussed by John Dewey in such works as *The School and Society* (Chicago: The University of Chicago Press, 1899) and *The Child and the Curriculum* (Chicago: The University of Chicago Press, 1902).

13   Evelyn Weber, *Ideas Influencing Early Childhood Education* (New York: Teachers College Press, 1984), pp. 33–103.

14   Ibid., pp. 104–91.

15   Descriptions of a wide variety of these programs can be found in Ellis D. Evans, *Contemporary Influences in Early Childhood Education* (New York: Holt, Rinehart & Winston, 1975).

16   Asa Hilliard III has made this point in several professional presentations, including that summarized in his keynote address to the annual meeting of the National Association for the Education of Young Children, Atlanta, Ga., 1983.

17   Frances E. Kendall, *Diversity in the Classroom: A Multicultural Approach to the Education of Young Children* (New York: Teachers College Press, 1983); Patricia G. Ramsey, *Teaching and Learning in a Diverse World* (New York: Teachers College Press, 1987); and Leslie R. Williams et al., *ALERTA: A Multicultural, Bilingual Approach to Teaching Young Children* (Menlo Park, Calif.: Addison-Wesley, 1985).

18   Evans, *Contemporary Influences in Early Childhood Education*, pp. 41–86, 193–326.

19   A recent development toward this end has been the commissioning of the Early Childhood Education Encyclopedia Project by Garland Publishing, Inc., of New York City. As one of the tasks in guiding the work, Leslie R. Williams and Doris P. Fromberg have assembled an editorial board representing a wide variety of early childhood involvements throughout the country. Each member of the editorial board is in turn contacting contributors for the preparation of articles, and some of the contributors are identifying other potential contributors. By the project's completion, it is likely that several hundred early childhood specialists across the United States will have been directly involved in the work. An obvious and important side effect of this activity continues to be the exchange of information and perspectives among the participants. Questions of delineation of the field, with examination of its inner structures and likely future directions, have assumed a central position in much of the resulting discourse.

20   Examples of such works are Bettye M. Caldwell and Asa G. Hilliard III, *What Is Quality Child Care?* (Washington, D.C.: NAEYC, 1985); and Deborah A. Phillips, ed., *Quality in Child Care: What Does Research Tell Us?* (Washington, D.C.: NAEYC, 1987).

21   Frances O'Connell Rust, with Valerie Malkus and Jane Romer, "The Teacher as a Curriculum Negotiator: Problem Solving in Mathematics as an Example," in *Teacher Renewal: Professional Issues, Personal Choices*, ed. Frances S. Bolin and Judith McConnell Falk (New York: Teachers College Press, 1987).

CONTRIBUTORS

SAMUEL J. ALESSI, JR., is currently acting assistant superintendent for curriculum evaluation and development in the Buffalo Public Schools. He is active at the local, state, and national levels in the Association for Supervision and Curriculum Development and the National Middle School Association. He is coauthor with James A. Beane and Conrad F. Toepfer of *Curriculum Planning and Development* (Allyn & Bacon, 1986.)

BARBARA T. BOWMAN is director of graduate students at the Erikson Institute, Loyola University of Chicago. She has worked with children and in teacher education both here and abroad and is past president of the National Association for the Education of Young Children.

BETTYE M. CALDWELL is Donaghey Distinguished Professor of Education at the University of Arkansas, Little Rock. She founded the Kramer Project, a comprehensive education and child care program, and is a past president of the National Association for the Education of Young Children.

JAMES P. COMER is Maurice Falk Professor of Child Psychiatry at the Yale University Child Study Center, associate dean for student affairs and director of the school development program, Yale University School of Medicine. He writes a monthly column for *Parents Magazine*. His professional interests include child rearing and development, school improvement, and race relations.

MARIAN WRIGHT EDELMAN, founder and president of the Children's Defense Fund, has been an advocate for disadvantaged Americans throughout her professional career. After receiving a law degree from Yale in 1963, she directed the Legal Defense and Education Fund of the NAACP in Jackson, Mississippi. In 1968, she founded the Washington Research Project, which in 1973 became the Children's Defense Fund.

DORIS PRONIN FROMBERG is professor of education and director of early childhood teacher education at Hofstra University and a former Teacher Corps director. She works with school districts on collaborative staff development and kindergarten curriculum. She is author of *The Full-Day Kindergarten* (Teachers College Press, 1987).

GUY P. HASKINS is currently supervisor of evaluation in the department of finance, research, and personnel of the Buffalo Public Schools. He is active in the National Staff Council, and in the American Educational Research Association.

SHARON LYNN KAGAN is associate director of Yale University's Bush Center in Child Development and Social Policy and is formerly director of the New York City Mayor's Office of Early Childhood Education.

PATRICK C. LEE is associate professor of education, Teachers College, Columbia University. The article in this issue of *Teachers College Record* is one of a series of essays he is currently writing on the social development of children in the early and middle childhood years.

RENÉE YABLANS MAGID is professor in the department of education at Beaver College, Glenside, Pennsylvania. She is coordinator of the early childhood administration program and the work-family program. She is also a consultant on balancing work and family to companies in the United States and abroad. Her current writings include coauthorship of *Exploring Early Childhood Education* (Macmillan, 1981), *Child-Care Initiatives for Working Parents: Why Employers Get Involved* (AMACOM, 1983), and *When Mothers and Fathers Work: Creative Strategies for Balancing Career and Family* (AMACOM, 1987).

DANIEL PATRICK MOYNIHAN is the senior United States Senator from the State of New York. He has served in the cabinets of Presidents Kennedy, Johnson, Nixon, and Ford. From 1973 to 1975, he was Ambassador to India and from 1975 to 1976 Ambassador to the United Nations. An author or editor of fourteen books, he was educated at Tufts University and The Fletcher School of Law and Diplomacy.

FRANCES O'CONNELL RUST is associate professor and director of the department of teacher education at Manhattanville College. Her involvement in early childhood includes founding and directing two preschool/kindergarten programs, teaching young children, and teacher education.

LISBETH B. SCHORR is lecturer in social medicine and member of the Working Group on Early Life, both at Harvard University. Her book *Within Our Reach: Breaking the Cycle of Disadvantage* was published by Anchor/Doubleday in May 1988.

LESLIE R. WILLIAMS is associate professor of early childhood education in the department of curriculum and teaching at Teachers College, Columbia University. Her interests include the history of the field of early childhood, the philosophies influencing its work, multicultural early childhood education, and infant study and practice. She is currently directing the preparation of an encyclopedia of early childhood education.

Index